Remember Me

by
Geraldine Smith
and
Donald Crawford

© 1996 The Young People's Church of the Air
and
Geraldine Smith

Special Thanks to Dean Crawford for designing the cover.

MS. GERALDINE SMITH

MS. GERALDINE IS A SPECIAL WOMAN.

SHE WAS THE ELEVENTH CHILD OF TWELVE. HER FATHER IS DECEASED. HER MOTHER IS 86 YEARS OLD, A WOMAN OF GREAT FAITH, WHO WAS MARRIED TO GERALDINE'S FATHER FOR 63 YEARS.

HER CHILDHOOD WAS SHAPED BY HER MOTHER, A DYNAMIC SPIRITUAL FORCE. SHE HAD A HEART OF GREAT LOVE AND HUMILITY. SHE TAUGHT GERALDINE DEEP SPIRITUAL TRUTHS. SHE DEMONSTRATED HER FAITH THROUGH HER LIFE AND STILL DOES TODAY. THEIR FAMILY GREW UP POOR, BUT RICH BEYOND MEASURE IN SPIRITUAL THINGS. THOSE EXPERIENCES BECAME THE FOUNDATION UPON WHICH GERALDINE'S SOLID CHRISTIAN FAITH NOW STANDS. THAT WISE OLD MOTHER LIVES ON TODAY, FULL OF WISDOM AND LOVE.

GERALDINE WORKED FOR MANY YEARS AS A SECRETARY AND GENERAL OFFICE MANAGER. SHE ALSO WORKED FOR THE COCA-COLA BOTTLING COMPANY, AND WAS AN EXEMPLARY WORKER. SHE WAS ALWAYS ACTIVE IN HER COMMUNITY AND HER CHURCH.

SHE DEVOTED CONSIDERABLE TIME TO THE ST. JUDE TABERNACLE AS A VOLUNTEER AND HELPED SO MANY IN NEED. SHE LATER BECAME AN ACTIVE MEMBER OF THE MT. OLIVE BAPTIST CHURCH.

AFTER HER INCARCERATION, SHE BECAME A GREAT HELPER, TEACHER AND FRIEND TO SO MANY WOMEN IN PRISON. SHE TAUGHT THEM TO READ, BUT MUCH MORE SO, SHE TAUGHT THEM VALUABLE LESSONS FROM THE HOLY BIBLE AND ABOUT CHRIST, HER SAVIOR.

MS. GERALDINE CONTINUES TO STUDY TO SHOW HERSELF APPROVED UNTO GOD, A WORKWOMAN, INDEED. SHE STUDIES AVIDLY, HAVING COMPLETED WORK FROM THE SALVATION ARMY, THE RHEMA, COURSES

FROM THE AMERICAN BIBLE ACADEMY, AND SHE IS PRESENTLY STUDYING FOR HER BACHELORS DEGREE WITH COURSES PROVIDED BY MARILYN HICKEY BIBLE COLLEGE AND THE UNIVERSITY OF BIBLICAL STUDIES AND SEMINARY IN OKLAHOMA.

THIS MOTHER AND SERVANT HAS LIVED BEHIND BARS FOR NINE LONG YEARS. AFTER ALL THAT TIME, SHE STILL AWAITS THE FINAL VERDICT OF THE ILLINOIS SUPREME COURT. THE FATE OF THE REST OF HER LIFE LIES IN THE HANDS OF THAT COURT AND GOD. 1996 IS A CRITICAL YEAR FOR MS. GERALDINE. SO MUCH WILL BE DECIDED. SO MUCH HAS HAPPENED TO HER THAT IS UNJUST AND UNFAIR. IT IS OUR HOPE, THE HOPE OF THOSE OF US WHO KNOW HER AND CARE FOR HER, THAT JUSTICE WILL BE DONE, AND THINGS WILL BE MADE RIGHT.

IN THE MEANTIME, SHE WITNESSES AND WORKS AT DWIGHT CORRECTIONAL INSTITUTE IN DWIGHT, ILLINOIS. SHE MINISTERS WITH WRITTEN AND SPOKEN WORD EVERY DAY FROM DEATH ROW. THESE ARE HER TESTIMONIES, HER WITNESS. HER HEART IN ACTION!

FORWARD

I MET HER BY CHANCE A YEAR AGO. I DIDN'T KNOW HER, HAD HEARD NOTHING OF HER.

A FRIEND WROTE ME AND TOLD ME THE STORY OF THE FIRST WOMAN ON DEATH ROW AT A PRISON IN THE STATE OF ILLINOIS. THE VERY FIRST WOMAN CONVICTED OF A CRIME AND SENTENCED TO DIE.

BUT EVEN MORE IMPORTANTLY, THAT WOMAN WAS A CHRISTIAN, SAVED BY GRACE. IN THAT DUNGEON OF DEATH, THIS DEAR LADY WAS A FIERY WITNESS FOR THE CHRIST SHE LOVED TO THOSE REJECTED AND FORSAKEN BY SOCIETY.

I WAS ASKED TO COME AND SEE FOR MYSELF. TO MEET HER, TO LISTEN TO HER TESTIMONY AND TO HEAR HER STORY. I REALLY DIDN'T WANT TO. I DIDN'T HAVE THE TIME. SHE WAS NO PART OF MY LIFE. THERE WAS SO MUCH ELSE TO DO, SO MANY OTHER PEOPLE TO TEND TO.

BUT I SOON REALIZED I HAD TO GO FOR I WAS CONVICTED DEEP WITHIN MY SOUL. IT WAS SOMETHING GOD WOULD HAVE ME DO WHETHER I WANTED TO OR NOT.

AND SO I WENT TO DWIGHT CORRECTIONAL INSTITUTE FOR WOMEN IN JOLIET, ILLINOIS WITH MY FRIENDS AND HERS, GLENDA LINER, KYLE SIMPSON AND REVEREND GOODWIN, HER PASTOR. I HAD RELUCTANTLY RESERVED ONE HOUR FOR OUR MEETING, PERHAPS TWO. I ENDED UP STAYING THE ENTIRE DAY.

AND SHE INDELIBLY ETCHED HERSELF INTO MY SOUL. SHE WAS A REMARKABLE WOMAN FULL OF JOY AND VITALITY. SHE WAS NOT BITTER, ANGRY OR RESENTFUL EVEN THOUGH SHE HAD EVERY RIGHT TO BE. SHE WAS FULL OF THE LOVE OF GOD.

BEFORE SHE WOULD TELL ME HER STORY, SHE TOLD ME HER TESTIMONY. SHE TOLD ME OF THE LOVE OF CHRIST IN HER LIFE BEFORE SHE TOLD ME THE PROBLEMS OF HER LIFE. GOD WAS ALIVE IN HER.

HER STORY THAT BROUGHT HER TO PRISON WAS HEART WRENCHING. SHE TOLD ME WHAT HAD HAPPENED AND WHY. WE DISCUSSED EVERY DETAIL, AGAIN AND AGAIN. SHE WAS AS OPEN AND HONEST AS ANY HUMAN BEING COULD BE. NOTHING WAS HELD BACK. I UNDERSTOOD HER AND WHAT HAPPENED TO HER.

IN SO MANY WAYS IT SEEMED SHE WAS BETRAYED. OUR LEGAL SYSTEM HAD FAILED HER. SHE HAD POOR AND IMPROPER REPRESENTATION AND A SERIOUS DEFAULT IN JUSTICE FROM OUR COURTS. NOTHING HAD BEEN DONE TIMELY. SHE HAD BEEN FORSAKEN, LEFT ALONE FOR MONTHS, EVEN YEARS WITHOUT HUMAN HELP OR HOPE. I RESOLVED TO HELP HER, TO DO WHATEVER I COULD TO HELP RIGHT THE WRONGS AND TO SEE THAT JUSTICE WAS DONE.

MS. GERALDINE IS A DEEPLY FEELINGFUL PERSON. HER SOUL IS RICH AND POETIC. SHE EXPRESSES HERSELF SO BEAUTIFULLY IN SO MANY WAYS. SHE HAS SENT ME WRITINGS FROM HER PRISON CELL, HER CEMENT COFFIN AS SHE CALLS IT, WHICH ARE UNIQUE TESTIMONIES OF THE CHRIST SHE LOVES. SHE WANTED MY HELP IN SHARING THEM WITH YOU. FOR ANYONE WHO READS THESE SPIRITUAL BLESSINGS CAN NEVER AGAIN BE THE SAME.

ALL THE THOUGHTS ARE HERS. THE TOPICS ARE HERS. MOST OF THE WORDS ARE HERS. I HAVE ONLY EDITED, ENLARGED AND ORGANIZED THESE PUNGENT THOUGHTS FOR HER. SHE WROTE TO ME IN PROSE. I HAVE TAKEN SOME AND TURNED THEM INTO POETRY. FOR HERS IS THE HEART OF A POET. HER TOPICS ARE VARIED. FROM RELIGION TO RACISM. FROM LOVE TO HATE. FROM FRAIL HUMANITY TO GOD ALMIGHTY. FROM PAIN TO MERCY. THESE ARE TESTIMONIES, DEVOTIONALS YOU WILL NEVER FORGET.

READ SOMETHING FROM HER EVERY DAY. IT WILL SPIRITUALLY ENRICH YOUR LIFE. THEY ARE WORDS OF ENCOURAGEMENT TO YOU FROM A WOMAN WHO NEEDS ENCOURAGEMENT AND HELP FROM YOU. THEY ARE WORDS OF LIFE AND JOY FROM A LIVING HELL. THEY ARE WORDS FROM A SISTER IN THE LORD TO ALL HER BROTHERS AND SISTERS. THEY ARE FROM A BLACK WOMAN TO PEOPLE OF EVERY COLOR AND KIND.

THESE ARE TESTIMONIES FROM A BLACK SISTER AND A WHITE BROTHER. WE ARE ONE IN HIM.

PRAY FOR HER.

HELP HER.

REMEMBER HER.

NEVER FORGETTING,

DONALD B. CRAWFORD

RELATE TO ME

RELATING IS MORE THAN A MERE VERBAL COMMUNICATION.

MUCH MORE THAN MERE WORDS.

MUCH MORE!

YOU MUST CATCH THE SINGLE TEAR IN MY EYE.

YOU MUST SEE THE SET OF MY JAW

AND READ ITS MESSAGE.

YOU MUST SENSE MY SHOULDERS SLUMP AND HEAR THEIR MESSAGE CLEAR.

YOU MUST HEAR EVERYTHING I <u>DON'T</u> SAY.

YOU CAN

IF YOU TOUCH MY SPIRIT AND I YOURS.

IF YOU HEAR THE NEVER SPOKEN WORDS OF MY HEART!

WORDS I CAN NOT SPEAK MYSELF.

THANK YOU FOR LISTENING.

THANK YOU FOR RELATING.

THANK YOU FOR KNOWING ME.

I THANK GOD FOR YOU!

REMEMBER ME!

SOLID GROUND ON DEATH ROW

I COME TO YOU FROM A LONELY PLACE.

DEATH ROW!

I AM ATTACKED BY LIFE'S HARSHEST FORCES.

EVERY DAY!

LIFE'S SEVEREST PAINS - ABJECT AGONY.

EVERY DAY.

MY HURT IS SO GREAT, MY PAIN SO SEVERE

I GO DEEP INTO MYSELF.

WAY DOWN DEEP.

WAY BACK TO MY CORE

TO MY SPIRITUAL ROOTS - MY SOUL!

THE COURSE OF MY LIFE IS LIFE'S HARDEST JOURNEY.

I FACE DEATH EVERY DAY - ON DEATH ROW!

FROM THIS DEPTH OF DESPAIR, FROM THIS AGONY, I <u>FIGHT</u>!

I FIGHT FOR MY CHRISTIAN VALUES,

FOR THE CHRIST I LOVE.

BUT I DO NOT FIGHT ALONE.

I AM CLOTHED IN THE FINEST SPIRITUAL ARMOR.

I CARRY THE ROD AND STAFF OF GOD ALMIGHTY IN MY FIGHT.

MY FEET ARE DIRECTED ON <u>HIS</u> PATH.

BY <u>HIS</u> SPIRIT.

I AM IN THE FRAY, IN THE FIGHT FOR THE RIGHT.

AND I AM CONTENT - FULFILLED!

OH THAT YOU MY BELOVED MAY SEE

THAT SUCH CHRISTIAN VALUES, SUCH SPIRITUAL LOVE

ARE SO MUCH MORE VALUABLE THAN COMFORT OR PLEASURE

AS I HAVE SEEN.

MY <u>HOME</u> ON DEATH ROW IS A BREEDING GROUND FOR FEAR.

BUT EVEN IN SUCH A PLACE WHERE MOST BELIEVE THERE CAN BE NO GOD

<u>HE IS HERE</u>!

HIS WORD LIVES IN THIS DUNGEON OF DEATH.

HIS SPIRIT IS WITH ME.

IT IS MY LIGHTHOUSE, MY GUIDE THROUGH THE STORM OF TRAVAIL AND TRIBULATION.

HIS SPIRIT AND HIS WORD ARE MY ONLY SOURCE OF COMFORT.

WITHOUT THEM, I WOULD BE <u>OVERCOME</u>.

BUT MY JESUS IS THE GROUND OF MY BEING.

IN HIM I REST MY EVERY WORRY AND GRIEF.

WITHOUT HIM I SINK IN SOUND.

BUT WITH HIM, EVEN ON DEATH ROW,

I STAND ON SOLID GROUND!

AND I WAIT.

SO PATIENTLY I WAIT.

I WAIT FOR GOD TO MAKE GOOD.

ON HIS EVERY PROMISE!

AND, IN FAITH, <u>I KNOW HE WILL</u>!

<u>HE</u> WILL REMEMBER ME.

MAY YOU REMEMBER ME!

BASKET OF PAIN

HOW I HURT!

SOMETIMES MY PAIN IS SO GREAT I CAN NOT BEAR IT.

AND THEN I CRY OUT!

HUMBLE CRIES, WITH HUMBLE TEARS.

I ASK HIM, I BEG HIM TO HELP ME UNDERSTAND MY PAIN.

HELP ME KNOW WHY MY LIFE IS AS IT IS.

TO TEACH ME.

TO TOUCH ME.

TO QUIET ME.

AND FILL ME WITH HIS SPIRIT.

TO GIVE ME AN EQUAL MEASURE OF LOVE

TO CALM THE AGONY IN THIS BASKET OF PAIN.

THAT IN THIS MY AGONIZING LONELINESS

FORSAKEN BY MAN

I WILL KNOW THAT GOD IS TRULY LOVE!

AND IN REPLY, HIS SPIRIT SPOKE

AND THAT KINDLY, HOLY GHOST SHOWED ME THERE IS MORE I MUST DO.

THAT I MUST BE OBEDIENT.

FOR IT IS ONLY WHEN I AM OBEDIENT IN MY PAIN

THAT GOD CAN WORK,

REPLACE MY PAIN WITH LOVE.

BUT WHEN I DISOBEY, WHEN I DEFY GOD, WHEN I DOUBT

I AM GROUND DOWN.

I AM BITTER.

MY SOUL WELLS UP WITH HATE

LOVE IS GONE!

AND THEN I SEE, SEE OH SO CLEARLY THAT

NO MATTER HOW GREAT THE SUFFERING, HOW LARGE MY PAIN,

AND WHAT I SUFFER DEFIES IMAGINATION

THAT HATE TURNS

AND IN MY ANGER, I QUESTION, I DEMAND REASONS-ANSWERS FROM GOD!

WHY? WHY? WHY?

AND I SEE THAT THE PAIN THE WORLD METES OUT WAS MEANT TO TURN US AWAY FROM GOD.

TO WEAKEN US SO THAT WE WOULD FALL PREY TO THOSE WHO GATHER TO HURT US.

IT IS SATANIC TESTING. IT'S PURPOSE IS TO DESTROY MY SPIRIT.

GOD WILL NOT HELP YOU IN THIS COFFIN OF DEATH.

THERE IS NO LOVE OF GOD HERE, SATAN SCREAMS!

AND IN THIS RAGING PAIN, RAGING HATE

MY SPEECH HAS NO VERSE.

MY ATTITUDE CORRUPTED AND NEGATIVE.

MY APPEARANCE UNKEMPT, DIRTY

I RESENT MYSELF AND OTHERS.

BUT THEN COMES A GLIMMER, THE FAINTEST RAY

OF FAITH, HOPE AND LOVE.

AND EVEN THAT SMALL LOVING BEGINNING STRENGTHENS ME.

AND I KNOW, I KNOW AGAIN SO SURE

THAT THE SOVEREIGN GOD I LOVE, WHO DIRECTS MY PATH, WHO PUT ME HERE

LOVES ME!

THE ONE WHO ALLOWS THESE RAGING STORMS

LOVES ME!

AND I LOVE HIM!

AND WHEN <u>HE</u> IS READY

MY GOD WILL REPLACE THE <u>RAGING STORM</u> WITH THE <u>COOLING BREEZE</u>.

IF I AM OPEN. IF I AM OBEDIENT. IF I PATIENTLY WAIT.

AND THEN I KNOW MY STAND IS STRONG.

SECURE.

EVERLASTING!

BECAUSE WITH ALL MY HEART, WITH ALL MY SOUL

I KNOW THAT GOD'S COOLING BREEZES WILL SOON COME.

I KNOW THIS.

I TRUST HIM.

I TRUST HIS WORD!

<u>AND I HOLD GOD TO HIS WORD!</u>

AND SO FROM DEATH'S ROW, I KNOW MY DUTY.

I MUST SHOW, I MUST LIVE THIS LOVE OF GOD.

FOR I AM HIS CHILD.

OBEDIENT TO HIS WORD AND HIS WILL.

<u>I AM A KINGDOM PERSON!</u>

IN LOVE.
NO MATTER HOW MUCH PAIN MAY BE BREWING IN MY BASKET OF PAIN,
   I WILL BE OBEDIENT
TO HIS KINGDOM DEMANDS.

AND I WILL <u>EXPECT</u> HIS EVERY BLESSING!

I WILL WAIT FOR GOD'S COOLING BREEZES WHICH I KNOW WILL COME.

THE KING'S KID

MY HERO

I HAVE A HERO.

MY HEART THROBS WHEN I THINK OF HIM.

HIS NAME IS JESUS!

HE WAS A HERO, THIS SON OF GOD.

HE WAS A LEADER. BUT HE ALSO SERVED.

HE WAS A LEADER <u>BECAUSE</u> HE SERVED.

HE WAS A LEADER BECAUSE HE WAS A SERVANT.

HE CAME TO DO FOR OTHERS - FOR ME!

AND SO I WOULD BE LIKE MY HERO, MY LORD

SO TOO I MUST SERVE!

AND I MUST SERVE AT THE LOWEST LEVELS

IF I WOULD LEAD.

AND SO IN MY LIFE,

I BECAME EMPTY AS A SERVANT.

I HAD TO.

SO THAT HIS SPIRIT WOULD FILL ME.

ENLIGHTEN ME.

ENABLING ME TO THINK, EVALUATE, TAKE STOCK AND LEARN.

I BECAME EMPTY SO THAT HIS PURIFYING FIRE COULD CONSUME THE CLUTTER IN MY LIFE!

<u>CONSUME ME</u>!

AND THEN A DIVINE POWER FLOWED WITHIN ME

FAR GREATER THAN ANY I HAD EVER IMAGINED

AND IT STOPPED MY SPIRIT FROM BLEEDING.

MY JESUS, MY HERO FED ME WITH HIS GRACE.

I WAS STRENGTHENED, ENERGIZED.

I COULD NOT FAIL OR FALL.

I WAS GUIDED, KEPT, MOTIVATED BY MY HERO.

AND I WAS FILLED WITH HIS PASSION.

AND EVEN THOUGH I LIVE EVERY MOMENT OF MY LIFE BEHIND BARS

I AM NOT OVERCOME!

I AM NOT OVERWHELMED!

FOR MY TRUST IS IN GOD, IN CHRIST MY LORD.

MY HERO!

AND I RELY ON MY HERO COMPLETELY, WHEN NO MAN IS NEAR.

I AM CONNECTED, ONE WITH HIS SPIRIT.

NO MATTER HOW DEMEANED AND DEBASED I AM

MY DIGNITY REMAINS!

NOTHING WILL CORRUPT IT!

I WILL NEVER FALTER!

I WILL NEVER BOW DOWN TO FALSE GODS!

MY STEP WILL NEVER WAIVER!

LOCK ME AWAY - PUT UP MORE BARS - INCREASE THE CHAINS OF BONDAGE

NOTHING

NOTHING WILL KEEP ME FROM THE LOVE OF GOD!

I WEAR THE CHAINS!

I REFUSE TO ALLOW THEM TO WEAR ME!

I WILL NEVER BE A PRISONER OF DARKNESS.

I WILL NEVER BE BOUND BY CHAINS.

I AM <u>FREE</u> IN CHRIST MY HERO!

I AM HIS AMBASSADOR.

I WILL BE EVERYTHING HE WOULD HAVE ME BE.

AND THOUGH DAY AFTER DAY AFTER DAY AFTER DAY

I AM ALONE, SO ALL ALONE WITH MY AGONIZING LONELINESS

I YET GO FORWARD AS

A WOMAN WITH PRIDE!

MY HUMANITY, MY DIGNITY STRONGER THAN EVER.

AND WHEN DEATH ROW HATES ME, I LOVE IN RETURN.

WHEN DEATH ROW TAKES,

I GIVE!

WHEN DEATH ROW HURTS, I COMFORT.

FOR I AM NOT HARD. I AM NOT HATEFUL. I WILL NOT BE MALICIOUS!

<u>FOR NO MAN CAN BREAK ME!</u>

DEATH ROW CAN NOT BREAK ME!

I AM A CHILD OF THE KINGDOM!

<u>THE KING'S KID</u>!

I AM A HERO BECAUSE JESUS IS MY HERO.

I ASK YOU AS KINGDOM PEOPLE TO RECOGNIZE ME AS I AM.

ONE OF YOUR OWN.

YOUR SISTER IN THE LORD!

YOUR FELLOW PRINCESS IN THE KINGDOM.

I STAND PROUD, POISED IN THE SHADOW OF MY HERO.

STAND WITH ME.

REMEMBER ME!

SHARING

I LIVE EVERY DAY WITH DEATH.

IT LURKS IN EVERY CORNER OF MY CELL.

IT YEARNS TO ENGULF ME,

TO SWALLOW ME UP.

I AM CONDEMNED AND I LIVE WITH THE CONDEMNED.

IN THIS MY DUNGEON OF DEATH,

DEATH ROW.

A BLAST OF LONELINESS BLOWS THAT CHILLS MY BONES.

EVERY HOUR OF EVERY DAY.

FACE TO FACE AM I WITH THIS LONELINESS UNTO DEATH.

BUT THEN I TURN TO JESUS.

I KNOW HIM WELL.

AND I LEAVE MY CELL

AND MOUNT UP UPON <u>HIS</u> WINGS OF LOVE.

AND WE SOAR IN BLISS TOGETHER

AND I USE THAT THRILLING TIME

ALONE WITH HIM

TO GROW IN LOVE, COMPASSION.

SO THAT WHEN I RETURN TO DEATH'S DUNGEON

WHAT I GET FROM HIM, WHAT I FEEL THROUGH HIM

ALLOWS ME TO BETTER LIVE MY LOVE FOR HIM.

MY WORLD HAS CAST ME ASIDE.

TO DIE!

I AM SENTENCED TO DEATH.

AND YET THE CLOSER THAT DAY COMES

THE NEARER I AM TO HIM.

I TRUST HIM AS I COULD NEVER TRUST ANYONE.

CHRIST'S WORDS ARE TRUE,

PERMANENTLY ETCHED IN MY HEART.

THEY TELL ME HE IS HERE, WITH ME,

AND I BELIEVE.

THEY TELL ME HE UNDERSTANDS MY PLIGHT AND I ACCEPT THAT.

FEAR NOT, SAYS HE, FOR I AM WITH YOU.

AND I BELIEVE THAT!

AND SO I SHARE WITH YOU FROM DEATH ROW MY PROMISE.

I WILL NEVER BREAK MY VOW OF TRUST TO THE SON OF GOD!

NOR WILL I EVER LOSE MY LOVE FOR HIM.

FOR MY ANGER IS GONE.

MY HATE ABATED.

FOR EVEN THOUGH MY NAME IS ON THE LIST,

DEATH'S LIST,

I THINK ONLY ABOUT LIFE, SPIRITUAL LIFE IN HIM!

AND I SEE THAT I AM IN HIS HANDS, IN HIS PLAN.

FOR I KNOW THAT EVEN ON DEATH ROW,

FOR ME TO LIVE IS CHRIST.

AND TO DIE IS GAIN!

AND BECAUSE OF THAT PROMISE, THAT HOPE

EVEN FROM THIS <u>HELL ON EARTH</u>

I SEND TO YOU ECHOES OF LOVE!

I SHARE WITH YOU THESE NUGGETS OF GOLD WHICH GOD HAS PLACED IN MY HEART.

I ASK YOU MY SISTER, I ASK YOU MY BROTHER,

THAT YOU RETHINK YOUR LIFE IN CHRIST

THAT WHEREVER YOU ARE, WHATEVER YOU DO

IT BE DONE AS UNTO HIM!

AND AS YOU REMEMBER THESE THINGS, AND HIM,

<u>PLEASE REMEMBER ME</u>!

MY PRIVATE SPIRITUAL MUSEUM

THE SPIRIT OF GOD IS MY TUTOR.

MY PRIVATE TEACHER TEACHES ME.

HIS TEACHINGS ARE INDELIBLY ETCHED ON THE WALLS OF MY HEART.

DIVINE ART!

AND THOSE DIVINE DRAWINGS MAKE UP MY PRIVATE SPIRITUAL MUSEUM!

AND EVERY DAY I ENTER MY PRIVATE MUSEUM.

AND EVERY DAY I HANG MORE AND MORE SPIRITUAL DRAWINGS ON THESE WALLS.

EVERY MOMENT I ETCH ANOTHER MEMORY.

ANOTHER SOMETHING SPECIAL BETWEEN GOD AND ME.

AND MY PRIVATE MUSEUM GROWS.

AND AS IT DOES, I AM ENLARGED, FULFILLED.

FULL OF LOVE.

AS I AM GIVEN, I WANT TO GIVE.

AS I AM LOVED, I WANT TO HELP.

AS HE IS KIND TO ME, SO AM I TO OTHERS.

AND I WANT SO PASSIONATELY TO COMMUNICATE THE LOVE I FEEL.

AND THOUGH I AM UNIMPRESSIVE IN SPEECH GOD GIVES ME WORDS, THOUGHTS, IDEAS, <u>PICTURES</u>.

TO SHARE WITH YOU FROM MY SPIRITUAL MUSEUM.

<u>KNOW</u> THIS ABOUT ME.

I <u>EXIST</u> ON DEATH ROW. I AM ONE CONDEMNED.

I AM THE FIRST WOMAN TO BE SENTENCED TO DIE IN THIS STATE!

PERHAPS YOU WOULD HEAR MY WORDS MORE CLEARLY HAD I DIED, MY TRAGEDY ENDED.

BUT HEAR ME NOW

WHILE I AM ALIVE, WHILE I AM WITH YOU

HEAR MY WITNESS OF LOVE, MY SIMPLE FAITH.

FOR IT IS REALLY THAT FAITH THAT KEEPS ME ALIVE, IN HOPE, IN LOVE.

MY FAITH IN CHRIST.

I PRAY THAT EVERY DAY

I MAY PAINT A PICTURE OF HIS LOVE FOR YOU

FOR ANYONE, FOR EVERYONE!

FOR AS THE MASTER ARTIST PAINTS WITH ME IN MY PRIVATE SPIRITUAL MUSEUM

I SHARE THAT SPIRITUAL ART WITH YOU

THAT YOU MAY SEE THE BRIGHTEST PICTURE OF HIS LOVE!

AND PLEASE REMEMBER ME.

AS YOU REMEMBER HIM TODAY.

PLEASE REMEMBER ME.

FORGIVENESS

WE ARE OUR ACTIONS.

WE ARE OUR WORDS.

THEY PROVE WHO WE ARE, WHAT WE BELIEVE.

THEY SHOW WHETHER WE HONOR OUR LORD. HOW WE LOVE HIM.

<u>BY THEIR FRUITS YOU WILL KNOW THEM</u>!

WE APPROACH GOD FOR FORGIVENESS.

IN PRAYER WE ASK FOR PENANCE.

BUT HOW READY ARE WE TO FORGIVE?

FOR CAN WE ASK FOR FORGIVENESS FOR OURSELVES WHEN WE ARE UNWILLING TO FORGIVE ANOTHER?

NO WE CAN'T!

FOR WHEN <u>WE</u> FORGIVE, <u>COMPLETELY FORGIVE</u>

BY THAT MEASURE WE ARE FORGIVEN.

THE MORE WE UNDERSTAND THE DEPTH OF GOD'S FORGIVENESS, HOW EASY IT BECOMES TO FORGIVE OTHERS.

EVEN OUR ENEMIES!

COMPLETELY FORGIVING OUR WORST ENEMY IS PROOF POSITIVE THAT WE HAVE BEEN FORGIVEN!

AND SO WE RELEASE, <u>WE LET GO</u>!

NO MORE BITTERNESS, NO MORE RESENTMENT.

WE RELEASE EVEN AS WE HAVE BEEN RELEASED.

WHAT A MARVELOUS CLEANSING. THE SLATE IS CLEAN!

NO MORE PRIDE. NOT OUR WAY BUT HIS WAY.

THE FORGIVING WAY!

OLD HATREDS ARE GONE.

THERE IS NO LONGER ANY THOUGHT OF REVENGE.

FOR IF THERE IS VENGEANCE, VENGEANCE IS <u>MINE</u> SAITH THE LORD!

FOR OUR PART, WE ARE FORGIVEN FAR MORE THAN WE DESERVE TO BE.

THE LEAST WE CAN DO IS TO DO UNTO OTHERS

TO FORGIVE AS WE HAVE BEEN FORGIVEN.

MEMORABLE AND ILLUMINATING MOMENTS

I FEEL SO DEEPLY.

I HAVE SO MUCH TO SAY. THERE IS SO MUCH DEEP INSIDE ME.

I FEEL LIKE A WELL WITH LIVING WATER.

TODAY MY SPIRIT SORES EVEN HIGHER THAN AN EAGLE.

IT RISES HIGH, FAR ABOVE MY PHYSICAL CHAINS OF BONDAGE.

MY HEART IS SO FULL

AS THOUGH I WERE SPIRITUALLY DINING AT THE LORD'S TABLE!

AND THE ENTREE THERE IS <u>TRUST</u>.

I WANT YOU TO KNOW, OH HOW I WANT YOU TO KNOW

THAT I TRUST GOD WITH ALL MY HEART

WITH ALL MY SOUL

WITH ALL MY MIND.

I AM FULL OF HIS LOVE AS I <u>EAT</u> HIS WORDS.

I AM SO FULL I CAN MEET THE NEEDS OF ANY HUNGRY SOUL.

BUT I WILL CONTINUE TO EAT AT GOD'S TABLE UNTIL MY CUP RUNNETH OVER

AND HOW I PRAY THAT MY DINNER WITH CHRIST AT HIS TABLE WILL NEVER END.

THE LOVE, THE SHARING, THE PEACE, THE FULLNESS AT HIS TABLE

HOW DELICIOUS!

I AM SO FULL OF HIS LOVE THAT I AM RELIEVED OF MY PAIN.

FOR MY PAIN IS SO GREAT MY SUFFERING SEVERE

IN THIS CEMENT COFFIN WHERE I AM CONDEMNED TO LIVE

BUT I AM SO FULL OF HIS LOVE, SO ENERGIZED I REACH OUT

AND I TOUCH

I SHARE THE FOOD FROM GOD'S TABLE WITH EVERYONE.

MY CUP RUNNETH OVER, MY SPIRIT FREE.

EVEN THOUGH MY BODY IS BEHIND BARS,

MY SPIRIT IS FREE. I AM FREE!

BUT WHEN I AM HUNGRY, WHEN I START TO HURT

THEN I RETURN FOR ANOTHER SPIRITUAL SUPPER

AND I AM ONCE AGAIN FILLED

AND MY FAITH IS ONCE AGAIN STRONG

MY DETERMINATION AFIRE.

FOR I AM A PERMANENT GUEST AT THE TABLE OF MY LORD.

AND I WILL DWELL IN HIS HOUSE FOREVER!

<u>REMEMBER ME!</u>

MY OFFERING

HOW I LOVE MY SAVIOR.

WHEN I THINK OF JESUS, HOW I YEARN TO WASH HIS FEET.

HOW I YEARN TO MINISTER TO HIM.

BUT I HAVE NO SWEET SMELLING PERFUME FOR HIM

TO BATHE AND CLEAN THE FEET OF MY SAVIOR

FROM DEATH'S ROW

NOR LONG LOCKS OF HAIR TO WIPE THOSE GODLY FEET CLEAN

FROM DEATH'S ROW

BUT I OFFER HIM ALL THAT I CAN

I OFFER HIM MY HEART, MY LOVE

AND I PRAY THAT HE UNDERSTANDS

THAT I BATHE HIS FEET AND CARE FOR HIM EVERY DAY IN MY HEART

I AM HIS SERVANT

I WOULD DO ANYTHING FOR HIM.

PROFILE OF A PLAIN LADY

WHO AM I?

A PLAIN LADY.

NO MORE - NO LESS,

SITTING ON DEATH ROW.

CONDEMNED

AND WAITING TO DIE.

I AM A WOMAN.

FRAGILE AND DELICATE.

THOUGH FRAIL, I POSSESS A GIANT MESSAGE!

AND YOU SHOULD KNOW THAT FROM THIS VALLEY OF DEATH

IN THESE WORST OF TIMES

I BRING YOU PEACE!

FOR THOUGH MY BODY IS IN SHACKLES, MY SPIRIT IS UNSHACKLED

THOUGH I AM BOUND, I AM FREE!

DEATH ROW HAS BEEN MY HOME FOR FOUR YEARS.

FOUR YEARS!

BUT I DO NOT SPEND MY TIME HERE FOR MAN.

I SERVE IT FOR THE MASTER OF EVERLASTING LIFE!

I SERVE MY TIME IN SPIRITUAL DELIGHT.

I SPEND EVERY PRECIOUS MOMENT OF MY TIME ON DEATH ROW

WITH HIM, MY JESUS!

FOR I HAVE NOT LOST THE BATTLE OF LIFE, BEHIND THESE BARS

I HAVE WON IT THROUGH HIM!

THE SHEPHERD WHO GUIDED KING DAVID IS MY SHEPHERD.

THAT VERY SAME LORD HAS RESTORED MY SOUL AS HE DID HIS.

I WALK THROUGH THE VALLEY OF THE SHADOW OF DEATH AS DAVID DID.

HE KNEW NO EVIL. NEITHER DO I!

FOR DAVID'S SHEPHERD AND MINE HAS KEPT AND RESTORED MY SOUL.

AND THOUGH I AM FRAGILE AND DELICATE,

THE LORD MY SHEPHERD IS WITH ME.

I FEAR NO EVIL!

FOR I KNOW THAT EVEN THOUGH I DWELL IN THE DUNGEON OF DEATH,

I WILL DWELL IN THE HOUSE OF THE LORD FOREVER!

SO I AM NOT PLAIN IN THE EYES OF GOD,

EVEN THOUGH I AM THE DAUGHTER OF A POOR FAMILY.

FINANCIALLY POOR.

THOUGH POOR, OUR FAMILY WAS SPIRITUALLY RICH!

MY FATHER WAS A TRUE PRAYER WARRIOR.

HE WAS A MAN HONEST AND SINCERE IN HIS RELATIONSHIP WITH GOD.

HE TALKED TO GOD, PRAYING. HOW MIGHTILY HE PRAYED.

AND MY MOTHER, MY MOM.

A STRONG, STURDY BELIEVER WAS SHE.

COMMITTED WITH PASSION TO HER JESUS.

SHE TAUGHT ME AND HOW I LISTENED.

AND I LEARNED THE THINGS OF GOD.

MY PARENTS LIVED THEIR FAITH.

THEY LED THEIR CHILDREN IN THE PATH OF RIGHTEOUSNESS AND LOVE.

THEIR LIFE WAS HARD BUT THEIR FAITH NEVER WAVERED.

AND THEN ONE DAY MY MOTHER CAME TO VISIT ME ON DEATH'S ROW.

I SAW HER AND I CRIED.

MOM CAME CLOSE TO ME AND SAID:

"IT'S O.K. TO CRY.

BUT WHEN THE TEARS ARE DONE LOOK UP TO HIM.

LOOK AHEAD.

<u>THE ONLY TIME YOU LOOK DOWN IS WHEN YOU ARE ON YOUR KNEES.</u>

WHEN YOU ARE ON YOUR KNEES BEFORE JESUS, YOU CAN'T STUMBLE, YOU CAN'T FALL!"

MY HEART AND SOUL WERE FILLED TO OVERFLOWING.

SUCH WISDOM FROM AN 81 YEAR OLD KINGDOM PERSON, MY MOM!

HOW MUCH SHE HELPED ME.

AND I SAW THAT THOUGH THIS STATE WOULD SLAY ME, YET LIKE JOB WILL I TRUST HIM!

I WILL NEVER LET GO. I WILL NEVER GIVE UP.

EVEN IF THE STATE SLAYS ME

IT CAN <u>NOT</u> KILL MY SPIRIT.

FOR MY HEART BELONGS TO HIM IN WHOM I HAVE BELIEVED.

I AM GRIPPED BY HIM.

HUGGED AND EMBRACED BY HIM.

HE HAS A PLAN FOR ME WHICH MAN CAN NOT KNOW!

AND I FIND NEW STRENGTH

AND THOUGH I FEEL BETRAYED AND FORGOTTEN ON DEATH ROW,

YET NEVER BY HIM!

NO MATTER HOW MUCH THE INJUSTICE, HOW EVIL THE MISTREATMENT,

I WILL FORGIVE AND I WILL FORGET EVEN AS HE HAS DONE THIS FOR ME.

FOR I AM NOT A VICTIM. I AM A VICTOR.

I WILL NEVER BE FORGOTTEN IF YOU

REMEMBER ME!

SURVIVAL

I SURVIVE.

SOMEHOW.

ON DEATH ROW.

I LIVE IN ACRES OF FRUSTRATION.

TROUBLE IS MY PORTION EVERY DAY.

MY LIFE IS ON THE LINE: MY LIFE!

I FACE MY DEATH THE STATE HAS DECREED EVERY DAY.

AND YET THROUGH IT ALL

I THINK OF <u>HIM</u>.

HIS DEATH.

HE DIED SINLESS FOR MY SIN.

HIS DEATH WAS THE BEGINNING OF MY LIFE.

ETERNAL LIFE.

A NEW LIFE, JOY UNSPEAKABLE.

HARD TIMES AND PERSECUTION ARE HERE AND WILL COME

AND YET I PRESS ON!

MY SPIRITUAL CANTEEN IS FILLED WITH THE LIVING WATER OF HIS ETERNAL LIFE.

MY BREAD IS MY FAITH IN HIM.

HIS LOVE IS THE MAP THAT GUIDES MY HEART.

EVEN ON THIS DEATH-DEALING TRAIL, I WILL SURVIVE!

TENDER AND FRAIL THOUGH I AM, HIS LOVE HAS MADE ME STRONG!

I AM STRONG ENOUGH TO HANDLE ANYTHING THIS WORLD METES OUT. BECAUSE OF HIM.

REMEMBER ME!

BLEEDING

I HEAR THE SOUND OF PAIN.

THE SOUND OF HURTING HEARTS

IN THIS VALLEY OF DEATH WHERE I LIVE.

I SEE THE TEARS OF THOSE LIKE ME

ABANDONED - FORSAKEN.

THEY SEARCH FOR HOPE. LIKE ME.

FOR LIGHT.

FOR DIRECTION.

FOR HOPE!

THEY CRY OUT FOR RELIEF

FOR ANYTHING THAT WILL STOP THE RESENTMENT

THE BITTERNESS, ANGER AND HATE

WHICH CORRODE THEIR VERY LIVES, THEIR SOULS!

AND WHEN I HEAR THE SOUNDS OF HURTING HEARTS,

WHEN I SEE THE PAINFUL TEARS

I REACH OUT AND TOUCH.

I OFFER MY LOVE, AND HIS LOVE TO THEM.

FOR HE ALONE CAN REPAIR AND RESTORE.

HE ALONE CAN STOP THE BLEEDING!

I KNOW!

FOR HE HAS STOPPED MINE.

I KNOW THE ONE WHO SUFFERED HIMSELF AND CAN STOP THE SUFFERING.

I CAN SHOW HIS LOVE.

WITH A SUNNY SMILE.

A CALMING COUNTENANCE.

A HELPFUL HUG.

A CARING CARESS.

I WILL <u>LIVE</u> HIS LOVE AND SHOW THEM.

I WILL FEED HIS SHEEP WITH THE NURTURING MILK OF HIS WORD.

EVEN FROM THIS FORSAKEN PLACE REMEMBERED OFTEN BY GOD ALONE MY LIFE WILL BE LIVING PROOF OF HIS LOVE.

FOR THE HURTING HERE ARE MY FRIENDS MADE IN THE IMAGE OF GOD.

LIKE ME. LIKE YOU.

FOR MAN HAS REGARDED MY FRIENDS AS WITHOUT WORTH AND DIGNITY.

BUT I KNOW THESE WOMEN MY SISTERS AND I LOVE THEM.

THEIR HEARTS BLEED, MY HEART BLEEDS.

I WILL SPIRITUALLY BANDAGE THEIR WOUNDS WITH ALL THE LOVE AND CARE I CAN.

<u>HE</u> AND I TOGETHER WILL DO EVERYTHING POSSIBLE TO STOP THEIR BLEEDING!

REMEMBER THEM!

REMEMBER ME!

KEEPER OF MY SISTERS

I LIVE ON DEATH ROW.

I AM A WOMAN.

I LIVE WITH OTHER WOMEN ON DEATH ROW.

OUR DEATH ROW HOMES ARE SEGREGATED.

WE ARE KEPT APART FROM OTHERS.

ONE DAY, A LADY LIKE ME ASKED ME TO SHARE WITH HER.

SHE TOLD ME SHE RESPECTED ME.

SHE CALLED ME MS. GERALDINE.

IT WAS HER WAY OF SHOWING RESPECT FOR ME.

I KNEW THAT THE RESPECT SHE HAD FOR ME

WAS THE RESULT OF CHRIST'S LOVE FOR ME

FOR THE CHANGE HE HAD MADE IN MY LIFE

FOR THE LOVE I HAVE FOR HIM!

AND I TOLD HER THAT.

AS I TESTIFIED, OTHERS BECAME QUIET AND LISTENED.

AND SOON THEY ASKED QUESTIONS.

THEY WANTED TO KNOW HOW I COULD BE SO STRONG, SO LOVING

AFTER LIVING ON DEATH ROW FOR FOUR YEARS!

AND AGAIN I SHARED. I SHARED GOD'S LOVE!

THE LOVE WHICH MADE ME STRONG.

IN AN ENVIRONMENT OF CRUELTY AND HATE.

AND THEY SAW GOD ALIVE IN ME AND IN THE WORDS I SPOKE.

ONE LADY SO FULL OF HURT AND ANGER SAID,

SHE BELIEVED GOD LOVED ME-MS. GERALDINE MORE THAN HER.

PRISON LIFE, SAID SHE, WAS ABOUT TO DRIVE HER INSANE!

I TOLD HER HOW MUCH GOD LOVED HER.

EVERY BIT AS MUCH AS HE LOVED ME!

WITH GOD THERE ARE NO FAVORITES.

SHE IS AS SPECIAL TO HIM AS I AM.

I SHARED THAT THE LOVE OF CHRIST IS AVAILABLE TO ANYONE

EVEN THOSE WHO LIVE IN DUNGEONS

LIKE WE DO.

AND FROM THAT DAY,

I KNEW THAT CHRIST WAS MORE REAL TO EACH OF THEM!

THAN EVER BEFORE!

REMEMBER THEM!

REMEMBER ME!

SCATTERING GEMS

I LOVE TO SCATTER SPIRITUAL GEMS.

HERE AND THERE.

ANYWHERE GOD LEADS.

LITTLE THINGS.

SPIRITUAL PEARLS FOR TROUBLED HEARTS AND MINDS.

HIS GEMS.

HERE IS ONE.

I THOUGHT SOMETIMES THAT JESUS STAYS SO HIGH UPON THE CROSS.

WE FORGET THAT HE WAS MAN AND MADE OF FLESH.

THAT HE LIVED AS WE LIVE.

THE HIGHER UP HE IS, THE MORE REMOTE

THE HARDER IT IS TO HEAR THE HEARTBEAT OF OUR LORD.

SHOULD WE NOT KNOW HIM AND LOVE HIM AS HUMAN TOO?

SHOULD WE NOT BE ABLE TO HEAR MORE OFTEN HIS HUMAN HEART BEATING

IN LOVE AND MERCY FOR HIS FELLOW MAN?

WE FOCUS ON HIS SPECIAL BIRTH,

A VIRGIN BIRTH.

OR HIS MIGHTY ASCENSION.

HIS TRIUMPH OVER DEATH AND THE GRAVE.

BUT SHOULD WE NOT ALSO RELATE TO THE CHRIST

WHO KNEELED AND PULLED AN UNCLEAN LEPER TO HIS BOSOM?

AND TO SEE HIM, THE CHRIST, GROANING IN THE SPIRIT AS MAN.

TO SEE HIM TROUBLED.

TO SEE HIM CRY AND WEEP AS ANY WOMAN DOES.

WE NEED TO KNOW THE CHRIST OF THE BIBLE IN HIS REAL LIFE!

AND IN OURS.

HE NEEDS TO BE AMONG US, IN US

AS BOTH MESSIAH AND MAN.

FOR WAS THE MAN JESUS NOT ILL AS WE OFTEN ARE?

WAS HE NOT HUNGRY AS WE HAVE BEEN?

WAS HE NEVER HOMELESS OR WITHOUT A PLACE TO SLEEP, AS WE HAVE BEEN?

WAS HE NOT IMPRISONED AS I AM?

DID HE NEVER DOUBT AS WE SEEM SO OFTEN TO DOUBT?

WAS HE NEVER LONELY AS WE ARE SO OFTEN LONELY?

DO WE REALLY SEE THE <u>SON OF MAN</u> AS HE REALLY WAS?

FOR SURELY HE HAS BEEN THERE,

LIVED AND FELT AS WE HAVE.

HOW CAN HE KNOW US AND LOVE US

IF HE DOES NOT UNDERSTAND US AS HUMAN BEINGS?

HOW CAN WE KNOW HIM AND TRULY LOVE HIM

IF WE CAN NOT IDENTIFY WITH HIS HUMANITY?

FOR HE WAS NOT MERELY AMONG US.

<u>HE WAS US</u>!

HE WAS JUST LIKE YOU AND ME.

WE KNOW FOR SURE THAT HE IS THE <u>SON OF GOD</u>.

BUT WE CAN NOT KNOW HIM

UNLESS WE ALSO KNOW WITHOUT A DOUBT

HE IS ALSO THE <u>SON OF MAN</u>!

DRINKING

I DRINK FROM A BITTER CUP.

HUMILIATION!

EVERY DAY.

BUT NO MATTER HOW BITTER,

I GROW IN THE NURTURE, THE ADMONITION AND WISDOM OF THE LORD.

<u>I LIVE IN HIS WORD</u>!

I DRINK FROM HIS CUP.

I DRINK SO MUCH I AM <u>SPIRITUALLY</u> INTOXICATED!

I AM SPIRITUALLY HIGH.

HIGH ON HIS LOVE AND INJECTED WITH HIS JOY!

I EAT AND DRINK WITH THE SPIRITS OF THE SONS AND DAUGHTERS OF THE LORD.

I STAND TOGETHER WITH THEM AS KINGDOM KIDS, CHILDREN OF THE LIVING GOD!

I DERIVE STRENGTH FROM THEM.

AND I SHARE THAT STRENGTH WITH YOU IN THESE WORDS.

MY TESTIMONY OF LOVE FROM THIS DUNGEON OF DOOM.

AND I AM STRENGTHENED

IF I KNOW THAT YOU CARE FOR ME.

I BEAR MY SOUL TO YOU.

HOPING YOU WILL HEAR MY CRY,

OPEN YOUR SOUL TO ME.

I TOAST YOU IN THE LORD!

<u>REMEMBER ME</u>!

GOD'S OUTLAW
ARMED AND DANGEROUS

I AM ARMED.

HEAVILY ARMED!

MY GUNS ARE MOUNTED AND LOADED.

I HAVE 39 CANNONS FROM THE OLD TESTAMENT!

I HAVE 27 CANNONS FROM THE NEW TESTAMENT!

I AM FORMIDABLE!

OF WHOM SHALL I BE AFRAID!

ARMED LIKE THIS, I FIGHT THE FIGHT OF FAITH.

I MOVE THROUGH THE ENEMY INVINCIBLE.

I GO THROUGH LIFE WITH THE WISDOM AND TEACHING OF 66 BOOKS!

I AM A BIBLE READING, BIBLE SEARCHING, BIBLE BELIEVING <u>SISTER</u>

GUIDED BY THE HOLY SPIRIT

COVERED BY THE GRACE OF GOD!

AND I ATTACK

<u>SATAN</u>!

MY ENEMY.

AND I DESTROY HIM WITH THE LOVE OF JESUS.

THERE IS NO GREATER WEAPON.

AND EVERY DAY IN DEATH VALLEY,

I RELOAD.

I REARM MYSELF FROM THE WORD OF GOD.

AND I AM A MORE POWERFUL SOLDIER THAN EVER

IN THIS BATTLE AGAINST SIN AND DEATH.

"THEY GOTTA GO!"

AND WHEN I WALK THROUGH THIS VALLEY OF DEATH ARMED AND DANGEROUS,

SATAN SHAKES IN HIS BOOTS!

AND WHEN THE BATTLE COMES,

WE WILL WIN BECAUSE WE ARE MORE THAN CONQUERORS.

I PRAY THAT YOU WILL ARM YOURSELF TODAY.

THAT YOU WILL MASTER THE WEAPONS FROM 66 BOOKS OF THE LIVING WORD OF GOD.

AND AS I STAND IN THE BATTLE FROM DEATH ROW,

SO MAY YOU STAND STRONG IN YOUR BATTLE

WHERE YOU ARE MY FRIEND.

FOR HIM!

STAND ARMED AND DANGEROUS,

ONE OF GOD'S OUTLAWS.

WITH ME!

REMEMBER ME!

PURPOSE IN THE HEART

MY SISTERS CAME TO VISIT ME TODAY.

ONE I DEEPLY LOVE SPOKE ONLY TO ME WHEN I SPOKE TO HER.

SHE SAT AND WATCHED

HER HEAD ON THE TABLE FOR THE MOST PART.

SHE SEEMED TO BE OBSERVING THE PAIN

THAT HAD DUG ITS WAY DEEP INTO OUR FAMILY LIVES.

MY FATHER, MY SISTERS TOLD ME

WAS HOSPITALIZED FOR SURGERY.

85 YEARS OLD!

OTHER BROTHERS AND SISTERS OF MINE WERE COMFORTING HIM.

MY SISTERS WERE FILLED WITH PAIN

ENGULFED LIKE ANGRY THUNDER CLOUDS WITH FISTS OF FIRE.

FOR 85 YEARS MY FATHER HAD WALKED WITH GOD.

ALL HIS LIFE.

AND OH HOW WE HIS FAMILY LOVED HIM.

AND RESPECTED HIM.

THE THOUGHT OF THE HEAD OF OUR HOUSEHOLD SO HELPLESS HURT
   SO DEEPLY.

AND TO THINK THAT MY DEAR FATHER FACING DEATH

KNEW THAT I TOO FACED DEATH ON DEATH ROW

WAS A THOUGHT TOO PAINFUL TO BEAR.

IN THAT DARKEST HOUR, THE LOVE OF GOD WAS THERE.

AND I SHARED WITH MY FAMILY.

LIFE IS NOT OURS, BUT <u>HIS</u>.

LIFE IS NOT ONLY TIME HERE AND NOW.

LIFE IS ETERNAL, FOREVER!

THE LIFE OF THE CHILD OF GOD NEVER ENDS.

FOR EVEN AS LIFE IS SACRED HERE AND NOW,

SO IT IS HEREAFTER.

AND I SHARED WITH THE DEAR SISTER I LOVE

HOPE WAS AMONG US! HOPE WAS OURS!

AND COURAGE CAME FORTH.

AND LOVE.

AND ANGER ABATED.

PAIN WAS RESOLVED.

THE LOVE OF CHRIST OVERCAME.

AND I FELT THE LOVE OF GOD IN ME RUB OFF ON THEM.

AND THEY WERE BLESSED, AND OVERCOME WITH HIS PEACE AND LOVE.

AND I KNEW THAT ALL THINGS WORKED TOGETHER FOR GOOD

TO THEM THAT LOVE <u>HIM</u>.

AND THAT GOD'S LOVE

WOULD BE <u>OUR</u> PORTION.

AND OUR FATHER'S AS WELL.

EVEN AS WE REMEMBERED HIM IN LOVE

REMEMBER ME!

EMPTY AND MISUNDERSTOOD

TO MY FRIEND.

THIS IS THE FIRST TIME I HAVE SHARED FROM THE DEPTH OF MY SOUL.

SOMETHING SO DEEPLY PERSONAL.

I DO SO BECAUSE I TRULY BELIEVE YOU ARE MY FRIEND.

MY <u>SOUL</u> MATE.

MY FOREVER FRIEND.

MAY 20, 1991.

I WAS SENTENCED TO DIE ON THIS DAY!

THE ONLY WOMAN EVER SENTENCED TO DIE IN THE STATE OF ILLINOIS!

I WAS ALONE. ALL ALONE.

IN UTTER ISOLATION.

I LIVED IN DEEP DEPRESSION AND UNIMAGINABLE DESPAIR.

I HAD NO ONE TO TURN TO. NO ONE.

NO CHURCH, NO PASTOR, NO FRIEND AT MY SIDE.

I HUNGERED TO BE COMFORTED, TO SHARE WITH SOMEONE, ANYONE!

BUT THERE WAS NO ONE!

NO ONE.

BUT THEN, MERCY.

IT IS FOUR YEARS LATER!

AND I AM HERE. I DID NOT DIE!

BUT YET ANOTHER DATE WAS SET FOR ME TO DIE,

EVEN SO, I THOUGHT NOT OF ME

BUT HOW I COULD HELP THOSE WHO LOVE ME

WHO FEAR FOR ME

PREPARE THEMSELVES FOR ME TO DIE!

AND A SIMPLE THOUGHT CAME.

A SONG!

YES, JESUS LOVES ME.

YES, JESUS LOVES ME. YES, JESUS LOVES ME. YES, JESUS LOVES ME. THE BIBLE TELLS ME SO!

IT WAS AS THOUGH IT CAME FROM HEAVEN AND THE ANGELS SANG!

AND I THOUGHT THAT THOUGH I WAS AT DEATH'S DOORSTEP,

IT WAS REALLY THE DOOR TO EVERLASTING LIFE!

FOR IF I WERE TO DIE, I WOULD LIVE IN HIM, WITH HIM FOREVER!

AND I WHO WOULD DIE BECAME STRONGER THAN ANY WHO WOULD NOT.

AND I THOUGHT ABOUT THOSE WHO WOULD SOME DAY KILL ME.

MY ENEMIES.

FOR THEM I HAD NO HATRED.

I WAS NEITHER BITTER NOR ANGRY.

MY HEART WAS FULL OF LOVE EVEN FOR THOSE WHO WOULD SLAY ME!

NO MALICE WITHIN. ONLY LOVE. GOD'S LOVE.

AND NOTHING WOULD SEPARATE ME FROM THAT.

NOTHING! NOT EVEN DEATH.

AND SO THE DAY TO DIE CAME AND WENT.

AND I AM STILL HERE!

LIVING WITH HOPE AND EVEN MORE LOVE FOR MY FELLOW MAN.

I AM FULL OF FORGIVENESS.

ON DEATH'S ROW, I LIVE ON IN HIS LOVE.

REMEMBER THAT.

REMEMBER ME.

THORNY IS THE ROAD

DEATH ROW!

A THORNY ROW.

THE KILLING FIELDS.

THE ROWS OF DEATH ROW GROW RAPIDLY.

JUSTICE IS SERVED THEY TELL US

WHEN THEY KILL US!

BEFORE 1991, THERE WAS NO DEATH ROW IN THE STATE OF ILLINOIS FOR WOMEN

NONE.

BEFORE ME.

I WAS THE FIRST.

BUT NOW, MORE OF THE GENTLE GENDER COME.

THE KILLING FIELDS SUPPLY THEMSELVES WITH MOTHERS AND DAUGHTERS FROM EVERYWHERE!

AND WHEN THEY COME, THEY ARE <u>ALL ALONE</u> LIKE ALL OF US ON DEATH ROW.

WAITING TO DIE.

FORSAKEN. FORGOTTEN.

LAMBS, ARE WE, READY FOR SLAUGHTER!

SO YOU SEE HOW MUCH WE NEED YOUR LOVE.

YOUR COMPASSION. YOUR UNDERSTANDING. YOUR HELP!

WE NEED <u>YOUR</u> LOVE!

FOR THEY WOULD KILL US.

BUT IS THERE EVER A RIGHT TO KILL?

EVER?

NO MATTER HOW HEINOUS THE CRIME?

THE GOD I LOVE AND SERVE SAID:

"THOUGH SHALT NOT KILL"

THERE WERE NO EXCEPTIONS.

THERE SHOULD NOT BE AN EYE FOR AN EYE.

BUT MERCY AND FORGIVENESS.

BUT DON'T KILL.

AND SO WE EXIST IN OUR CEMENT COFFINS

CONDEMNED GRAVEYARDS

WONDERING WHETHER THEY WILL KILL US.

THE THOUGHT OF DEATH IS EVERYWHERE

AND DEPRESSION, AND DESPAIR.

BUT THE VERDICT STAYS FIRM.

"YOU ARE CONDEMNED!"

"WE WILL SLAY YOU".

BUT FOR ME, EVEN THOUGH I KNOW THAT,

KNOW THEY WOULD KILL ME,

YET WILL I TRUST HIM!

AND YOU, MY FRIEND, WHAT ABOUT YOU?

WILL YOU TRUST HIM?

NO MATTER WHAT? EVEN IF YOU FACE DEATH?

HE WILL BE THERE TO COMFORT YOU.

HE WILL SUPPORT YOU.

AND <u>THEN</u> WILL YOU BE THERE FOR ME?

AND <u>YOU</u>, WILL YOU COMFORT ME?

SUPPORT ME?

WILL YOU REALLY BE THERE FOR ME?

WILL YOU COME AND SEE ME?

<u>WILL YOU REMEMBER ME?</u>

SMORGASBORD OF DELIGHT

I WAS TERRIFIED,

WHEN I FIRST CAME TO PRISON.

ABSOLUTELY TERRIFIED!

I FOUND ONE WHO HAD BEEN THERE, WHO KNEW

AND I SHARED WITH HER MY FEARS.

AND SHE TOLD ME WHAT SHE KNEW.

PRISONS HARBOR EVIL.

THERE IS VIOLENCE

STEALING

RAPE

HOMOSEXUALITY

DRUG ABUSE

GANGS

AND MORE. MUCH MORE.

THERE ARE NO SUCH THINGS AS HUMAN RIGHTS.

AND THERE ARE THOSE WHO MERELY PROFESS A BELIEF IN GOD

HYPOCRITES ARE THEY FOR THEY PRACTICE NOT WHAT THEY PREACH.

BUT NO ONE STANDS UP, NO ONE CONDEMNS, NO ONE CONFRONTS.

NO ONE!

WHY? FEAR!

EVERYONE IS AFRAID.

AND FEAR PARALYZES.

THOSE WHO TREMBLE IN FEAR HAVE NO COURAGE.

SO MANY WOMEN ARE SUBMISSIVE, AFRAID.

IN PRISON, THEY DO NOT HAVE THE COURAGE TO STAND UP FOR THEMSELVES.

SOME HAVE BEEN BATTERED AND BRUISED, OUT THERE.

VICTIMS OF VIOLENCE.

AND THEY FEAR VIOLENCE, RETRIBUTION.

AND SO THEY ARE PASSIVE, QUIET

NO MATTER WHAT.

EVEN WITH POOR FOOD.

INADEQUATE MEDICAL CARE.

ARBITRARY PUNISHMENTS.

RACISM.

INADEQUATE EDUCATION.

AND MORE.

SOME COMPLAIN OF THEIR HURT AND PAIN

THE REMEDY OFFERED SO OFTEN IS DRUGS. EVEN IN PRISON.

DRUGS SOLVE NO PROBLEMS!

LIFE HERE SEEMS CHEAP, OF SUCH LITTLE VALUE.

A BATTLE TO BE FOUGHT EVERY DAY.

BUT WRONGS MUST BE MADE RIGHT.

AND IN HERE. OUT THERE. THE BATTLE MUST BE FOUGHT OUT THERE AS WELL.

YOU, <u>YOU</u> MUST HELP! HELP US!

THE CHURCH OF CHRIST MUST HELP.

YOU MUST FIGHT FOR US, FOR CHANGE

IN HERE.

YOU OUT THERE - WE IN HERE. TOGETHER FOR EACH OTHER!

HOW DESPERATELY WE IN HERE NEED YOUR HELP.

DON'T TURN YOUR BACK ON US.

PLEASE DON'T.

HELP US!

WE ARE HUMAN BEINGS.

STILL!

GOD LOVES US. STILL!

YOU SHOULD LOVE US. NO MATTER.

AND HELP US!

AND REMEMBER US!

A STRANGER
MY FRIEND, MY BROTHER

I HAVE A NEW RELATIONSHIP. A NEW FRIENDSHIP.

FORGED BY HONESTY

WRAPPED WITH THE ARMS OF GODLY LOVE

THE RELATIONSHIP IS STRONG. IN HIM.

IT WILL NEVER FADE. BECAUSE OF HIM!

MY FRIEND MADE A DIFFERENCE FOR ME.

HE CAME TO VISIT ME.

A STRANGER.

I NEVER EXPECTED HIM.

AND YET I SENSED HIS COMING AND I SENT THIS MESSAGE:

<u>COME AND SEE</u>!

I KNEW HE WOULD.

TWO STRANGERS SAT ACROSS A TABLE

AND BEGAN TO BUILD A MASTER PLAN.

THE BOND WAS CHRISTIAN LOVE.

GOD GAVE ME COURAGE TO BARE MY HEART.

SO DIFFICULT FOR ME.

I KEPT NO SECRETS, NO MASKS, NO HYPOCRACY.

I TOLD HIM MY <u>BITTER</u> STORY

WITHOUT BITTERNESS.

WE SHARED OPENLY

A FRIENDSHIP WAS BUILT.

MY FRIEND, THE STRANGER, SAW MY HONESTY AND OPENNESS.

HE NEVER JUDGED ME. HE ACCEPTED ME IN CHRISTIAN LOVE.

HE BROUGHT HOPE TO ME.

A VESSEL CRACKED AND BROKEN.

HE SAW THE VALUE IN ME. WHAT JESUS HAD DONE IN ME.

MY FRIEND WAS STRAIGHT, HONEST,
DEMANDING FACT AND TRUTH AT ALL TIMES.

THERE WAS NOTHING BUT THAT BETWEEN US.

AND BECAUSE OF THAT

MY FRIEND WILL STAND BESIDE ME.

HIS LOVE IS A CONSTANT REMINDER

TO KEEP MY EYES ON CHRIST.

LIKE BURNING LIGHT WITHIN LIGHT

HE BRIGHTENS THE COUNTENANCE OF THIS LONELY WOMAN.

HE ENCOURAGES, BUILDS AND QUIETLY PLACES KINGDOM NUGGETS IN ALL THE RIGHT PLACES.

HE STANDS BETWEEN ME AND THE CROWD POISED TO JUDGE.

POISED TO DO ME IN.

TO KILL!

HE KNOWS MY SUFFERING AND HE WILL HELP ME.

WE HAVE A COMMON LOVE FOR HIM WHICH WILL NEVER FAIL.

HE IS MY BROTHER, MY BELOVED IN THE LORD.

MY FRIEND IN DEEDS.

HE REMEMBERS ME.

AND YOU

WILL YOU REMEMBER ME?

WHO ARE YOU?

I DO NOT LIKE TO TALK ABOUT MYSELF.

HOW I WISH I LIVED AN AVERAGE LIFE, IN AN AVERAGE PLACE.

BUT MY HOME IS DEATH ROW. A SPECIAL PLACE.

GOD HAS A REASON FOR THAT.

EVEN HERE, IN DEATH'S DUNGEON, THIS FORSAKEN PLACE, GOD DOES WONDROUS THINGS FOR ME.

I STORE THEM DEEP INSIDE

SO THAT I CAN SHARE THEM.

ONE DAY I HAD AN ENCOUNTER.

A LADY I NEVER KNEW ASKED ME WHO I WAS.

I TURNED AND LOOKED AT HER.

AND AS OUR EYES MET, SHE SAID:

"YOU ARE HERE TO HELP US!"

AND I REALIZED THAT GOD HAD GIVEN ME ANOTHER OPPORTUNITY.

TO SHARE HIS LOVE.

AND I WAS ABLE TO SERVE HER A <u>FEAST</u> OF FAITH.

SHE ASKED HOW I, CONDEMNED TO DIE, COULD BE OF SUCH FAITH.

I TOLD HER I WAS IN LOVE.

I SHARED MY LOVE FOR JESUS CHRIST, MY SAVIOR.

HE WHO WASHED MY SINS.

I SHARED HOW HARD IT IS TO <u>LIVE</u> A LIFE OF FAITH.

IN HERE.

IT IS SO EASY TO TALK ABOUT IT.

BUT GOD'S DEEP LOVE MOTIVATES US TO LIVE THAT LIFE.

NO MATTER HOW HARD.

GOD IS LOVE IS SO TRUE, SO AVAILABLE TO EVERYONE.

EVEN IN HERE.

AND EVERY DAY THAT LOVING FAITH IS TESTED.

AND THEN WE FIND OUT HOW MUCH GOD REALLY MEANS TO US AND WE TO HIM BY HOW WE ACT.

AS WE STAND TALL, WE ARE A WITNESS TO ALL.

I WAS TO HER.

SHE FELT MY FAITH IN ACTION.

SHE SAW GOD'S PEACE IN MY DEMEANOR.

SHE SAW GOD'S LOVE IN MY EYES.

FOR TWO HOURS I SHARED GOD'S LOVE AND SHE LISTENED.

AND I LISTENED TO HER, HER CRIES, HER ANGER, HER DESPAIR.

AND AT THE END, THERE WAS HOPE.

SHE SAW THE REAL JESUS FOR THE FIRST TIME.

GOD'S BABIES

I SHARE OFTEN TO YOUNG FEMALE PRISONERS.

ALWAYS ABOUT JESUS

HIS DEATH, HIS RESURRECTION, AND HIS SAVING LOVE.

WHAT, THEY ALWAYS WONDER, WOULD THE LIFE AND DEATH OF JESUS HAVE TO DO WITH A YOUNG PERSON.

THAT STUFF IS FOR OLDER PEOPLE, THEY THINK.

THEY TELL ME, THESE YOUNG PEOPLE DO,

THEY CAN NOT RELATE TO THE BIBLE AND ITS MESSAGE.

THEY WANT MODERN EXAMPLES,

SOMETHING THEY CAN RELATE TO.

BUT I TELL THEM HOW GOD USED SO MANY YOUNG PEOPLE.

YOUNG PEOPLE RELATED TO HIM.

SO MANY OF GOD'S BABIES WERE EXAMPLES IN ACTION.

JESUS AT TWELVE YEARS OF AGE ASTOUNDED THE SCHOLARS IN THE TEMPLE.

DAVID THE YOUNG MAN SLEW THE MIGHTY GIANT GOLIATH.

JOSEPH THE TEENAGER THROWN INTO A PIT BECAME A LEADER OF EGYPT.

DANIEL, A YOUNG SERVANT OF GOD, SLEPT SAFELY WITH LIONS.

THE WORD OF GOD WAS ALIVE AS FIRE IN THE BONES OF YOUNG JEREMIAH.

THE BEAUTIFUL YOUNG VIRGIN, ESTER RISKED HER LIFE FOR HER PEOPLE.

CHRIST RESTORED THE DEAD TWELVE YEAR OLD DAUGHTER OF JAIRUS TO LIFE.

A YOUNG WOMAN WAS CHOSEN BY GOD TO BE THE MOTHER OF HIS SON.

MOSES THE BABY WAS PUT AMONG THE BULRUSHES AND GREW TO BE ONE OF GOD'S GREATEST PROPHETS.

AND SO MANY MORE.

ALL WERE YOUNG, VERY YOUNG.

YET HOW MIGHTILY THEY WERE USED OF GOD.

AGE IS IRRELEVANT TO GOD.

OUT OF THE MOUTHS OF BABES OFTEN COMES PROFOUND WISDOM.

I FELT SUCH LOVE FOR THESE YOUNG LADIES

SO DESPERATELY IN NEED OF THE LOVE OF CHRIST.

AND I PRAYED THAT I MIGHT MOTIVATE THEM BY MY EXAMPLE.

FOR THEY ARE THE JEWELS, THE YOUNG JEWELS OF HIS KINGDOM.

THEY ARE OUR FUTURE AND GOD'S PRESENT.

REMEMBER THEM.

REMEMBER ME.

UNSEEN TEARS AND WEEPING HEARTS

IN MY DUNGEON OF DEATH AND GRIEF

I SEE SO MANY TEARS.

I HEAR HEARTS WEEPING. MOTHER'S HEARTS.

I SEE MOTHERS IN PRISON

PASSIONATELY YEARNING FOR THEIR CHILDREN LEFT BEHIND.

CHILDREN THEY SO DEARLY LOVE.

SO MANY OF THESE MOTHERS

FEEL SUCH GREAT REMORSE

FOR THE CRIMES THEY HAVE COMMITTED AGAINST SOCIETY.

THEY KNOW THEY MUST PAY THEIR DEBT.

BUT WHILE THEY DO,

THEY DESPERATELY WANT TO BETTER THEMSELVES FOR THEIR LIFE AHEAD.

TO GROW.

BUT THEY HURT SO DEEPLY SO OFTEN

THEY KNOW HOW UNFORGIVING PEOPLE CAN BE.

HOW HURTFUL.

SO MANY ARE FORSAKEN AND FORGOTTEN.

THE PAIN OF THIS REJECTION IS SO HARD TO BEAR.

MANY HAVE HAD TO BE MOTHERS TO THEIR CHILDREN

WITHOUT FATHERS.

THEY HAVE HAD TO DO TOO MUCH.

THESE GIVING MOTHERS NURTURED AND LOVED THEIR CHILDREN

WITHOUT THE HELP AND LOVE OF A FATHER.

AND NOW THEIR CHILDREN ARE DEPRIVED OF THE LOVE OF THEIR MOTHER

THE ONLY LOVE THEY HAVE EVER KNOWN.

OH HOW THESE MOTHERS WEEP

LIKE RACHEL OF OLD

FOR THEIR CHILDREN.

THEY CRY OUT DESPERATELY FOR THEIR BABIES.

CAN IT BE RIGHT, CAN IT BE JUST

THAT A MOTHER WHATEVER SHE DID

WOULD BE SEPARATED FROM HER BABY?

IT GOES AGAINST THE WISHES OF GOD.

THE BONDING IN LOVE OF MOTHER AND CHILD SHOULD NOT BE BROKEN.

GOD KNOWS THAT SO WELL

FOR HE GAVE US <u>HIS SON</u>.

THAT BABE WAS NURTURED BY THE LOVE OF MARY, HIS BELOVED MOTHER.

NOTHING SEPARATED HER FROM HIM.

I KNOW THAT MOTHER'S LOVE.

I AM AN INCARCERATED MOTHER.

I AM SEPARATED FROM MY CHILDREN.

I HURT, OH HOW I HURT.

THERE ARE TIMES I AM WRACKED WITH PAIN.

I SO DESPERATELY SEEK THE LOVE OF MY CHILDREN

AND TO FEEL THEIR LOVE FOR ME.

HOW MY HEART ACHES, HOW IT WEEPS. FOR THEM.

WHEN YOU REMEMBER ME, WEEP FOR ME AS I WEEP FOR THEM.

PERHAPS YOU, WHILE WE MOTHERS ARE HERE, AWAY FROM THEM, COULD LOVE THEM FOR US.

PLEASE REMEMBER THEM

AND PLEASE REMEMBER MOTHERS HERE

AND MOTHERS, REMEMBER ME!

OUT MUSCLING MEANNESS

A YOUNG FEMALE PRISONER ESCAPED IN MAY 1995.

SOON SHE WAS CAPTURED AND RETURNED.

HER FELLOW PRISONERS SCORNED AND RIDICULED HER

BECAUSE HER ESCAPE HAD CAUSED THE PRISON TO BE ON LOCK-DOWN FOR THREE DAYS.

SOON AFTER, I SAW A LADY SITTING IN A LOCKED CONFERENCE ROOM

HER BACK TURNED

HER HEAD SLUMPED.

GOD MOVED ME TO REACH OUT TO HER.

I KNOCKED ON THE GLASS

WITH MY HANDCUFFS.

SHE TURNED

AND I SAW PAIN, SO MUCH PAIN.

A DESPERATE NEED FOR CARING. FOR LOVE.

I TOLD HER I CARED.

NO MATTER WHAT SHE DID, I CARED!

SHE TURNED AWAY AND THEN LOOKED BACK,

TEARS STREAMING DOWN HER FACE.

AGAIN, I LOOKED HER IN THE EYE

AND TOLD HER THAT I CARED!

AND I TOLD HER THAT CHRIST CARED FOR HER

AND THAT SHE WAS NOT ALONE.

AND THEN SHE SMILED THROUGH HER TEARS.

AND I ENCOURAGED HER TO CRY.

AND THEN I ASKED THE GUARD IF I COULD GIVE HER A HUG

A SIMPLE HUMAN HUG.

BUT SHE SAID NO.

SINCE THAT PRECIOUS TIME, I HAVE SPOKEN WITH HER OFTEN.

EACH TIME I TELL HER

HOW MUCH I LOVE HER IN CHRIST.

AND HOW MUCH CHRIST LOVES HER.

MY FRIEND WAS BLACK, AFRICAN-AMERICAN.

ALL OF THE FEMALE PRISONERS IN SEGREGATION UNITS ARE BLACK EXCEPT TWO.

I AM BLACK

AND I UNDERSTAND HOW DIFFICULT IT WAS FOR THIS YOUNG, BLACK LADY.

I COULD RELATE TO HER,

AND SHE TO ME.

I ENCOURAGED AND I EMBRACED HER.

BUT I ALSO GAVE HER REPROOF AND CORRECTION.

I WAS STRAIGHT WITH HER.

WHATEVER I SAID, SHE KNEW I CARED.

FOR WHEN IS SEE EVIL, I WILL SAY SO.

AND I WILL WAGE WAR AGAINST THAT EVIL.

I WILL RESIST WITH ALL MY MIGHT, <u>EVEN IN HERE</u>.

FOR I KNOW GOD LOVES EVERYONE IN HERE.

AND HATES EVIL.

OH HOW I PRAY SO OFTEN

THAT GOD'S LOVE WOULD MEND THE BROKEN HEARTS OF THOSE IN PRISON.

WE THE FORSAKEN AND FORGOTTEN.

WHEN I FEEL ALONE,

ALL ALONE

I STRAP UP MY CHRISTIAN BOOTS

AND WALK THOSE EXTRA SPIRITUAL MILES

FOR THOSE IN NEED OF LOVE AND CARE.

IN LOVE, I WILL BE AN EXAMPLE FOR THE JESUS I LOVE.

EVEN WHEN I AM TIRED, AND SOMETIMES I AM SO TIRED

I ASK GOD FOR STRENGTH TO DO MORE,

AND MORE,

AND EVEN MORE!

I AM, I SAY TO MY LORD, ALWAYS AVAILABLE.

I WILL GO WHERE YOU LEAD ME.

I WILL FEED YOUR SHEEP WHEREVER I FIND THEM.

I WILL ALWAYS FLEX MY SPIRITUAL MUSCLES.

EVEN ON DEATH ROW!

ESPECIALLY ON DEATH ROW!

REMEMBER THAT.

REMEMBER ME!

THE FORCE WITHIN

I LIVE THE LIFE OF THE SPIRIT.

I HAVE NO CHURCH.

I HAVE NO MINISTER.

I HAVE NO CONGREGATION OF BELIEVERS.

MY CHURCH IS THE FELLOWSHIP OF GOD'S HOLY SPIRIT DAY BY DAY.

EVERY DAY I REACH DEEP INSIDE FOR THAT SPIRITUAL FORCE WITHIN ME.

AND I GROW EVERY DAY IN HIS HOLY SPIRIT.

I GROW IN UNDERSTANDING AND WISDOM.

IN IMAGINATION, FAITH, LOVE,

WILL, STRENGTH, DISCIPLINE AND ZEAL.

FOR ALL OF THAT IS IN ME.

GOD-GIVEN,

ENERGIZED BY THE SPIRIT OF GOD.

I AM REQUIRED TO USE THOSE PRECIOUS THINGS WHICH GOD HAS GIVEN ME

FOR HIS GLORY.

THEY ARE DEEP, LASTING, PERMANENT, IN ME.

AS HE IS.

THEY ARE WHAT A CHRISTIAN IS! SHOULD BE.

WITH THEM, I AM IMPERVIOUS TO THE ENEMY!

I CAN RESIST EVIL,

TESTIFY FOR GOD IN BOLDNESS AND CONFIDENCE.

MAY YOU REACH DEEP INSIDE TODAY

TAP THE ENERGIES OF THE SPIRITUAL FORCE WITHIN YOU.

AS I DO.

REMEMBER ME.

THE STORY OF A SOUL

A LADY, MY FRIEND, HAS BEEN ON DEATH ROW FOR THREE YEARS.

WITH ME.

SHE APPEALED HER SENTENCE TO DIE.

THE HIGH COURT DENIED HER.

SHE CAME TO ME FOR HELP.

SHE BELIEVED SHE COULD TRUST ME

WITH THE MASSIVE PAIN WHICH ENGULFED HER.

SHE WALKED ME THROUGH HER LIFE.

SHE SHOWED ME HER PAIN

THE ABUSE, CONFUSION AND PROBLEMS WHICH SHE EXPERIENCED.

SHE TOLD ME THERE WAS NO MORE FIGHT WITHIN HER.

SHE HAD ENOUGH.

IT WAS TIME FOR HER TO QUIT, TO GIVE UP.

IT WAS TIME FOR HER TO DIE!

I LISTENED LOVINGLY.

I FOUND MYSELF ASKING GOD NOT TO PUT ANOTHER BURDEN ON ME.

I FELT SO TIRED, SO OVERLOADED

I SHARE THE PROBLEMS OF SO MANY, SO MANY.

EVERY DAY.

I FELT I SIMPLY COULD NOT MUSTER THE STRENGTH TO HELP HER.

AND I WONDERED WHETHER ANYONE REMEMBERED

THAT I TOO AM FACING THIS VERY SAME DEATH!

THAT I HAVE THE SAME PROBLEMS. AS SHE.

THAT I HURT.

THAT I AM ALONE!

THAT I NEED SOMEONE, FOR ME!

BUT I KNEW I WOULD HELP HER.

GOD REQUIRED THAT.

MY FRIEND NEEDED SO MUCH.

AND SO I ASKED GOD TO GIVE ME THE STRENGTH TO HELP HER.

AND HE DID.

AND I FELT REFRESHED,

ENERGIZED BY HIS SPIRIT.

AND I REJOICED

IN THE STRENGTH GOD GAVE ME.

WHEN MY FRIEND HAD FIRST COME TO DEATH ROW,

I HAD GREETED HER WARMLY AND SHARED MY FEW PERSONAL FOOD AND HYGIENE ITEMS WITH HER.

ONE DAY AS I SAT WITH BOOKS AND PAPERS

ABOUT MY TRIAL,

SHE ASKED WHAT I WAS READING.

I TOLD HER IT WAS WHAT THE JUDGE HAD SAID ABOUT ME.

WHEN HE SENTENCED ME.

I READ THE ENTIRE STORY TO HER.

AND WHEN I WAS THROUGH SHE CRIED OUT:

"WHAT THE HELL, IS THAT ALL?"

I SAID A SIMPLE YES

AND SHE STARED AT ME IN SHOCK.

THEN SHE STORMED OUT OF MY ROOM

AND RETURNED WITH HER OWN TRANSCRIPT, SOME TWO INCHES THICK!

HER JUDGE HAD DESCRIBED HER AS AN EVIL CREATURE.

FOR SEVENTEEN PAGES!

HE PAINTED HER AS A MONSTER FOR THE CRIMES SHE COMMITTED.

FOR ANOTHER FIFTY PAGES!

AND SHE STORMED FROM MY ROOM.

I WENT AND FOUND HER SITTING IN A CORNER CRYING.

SHE LOOKED AT ME WITH TEARS IN HER EYES AND SAID:

"MS. GERALDINE, WHAT THE HELL ARE YOU DOING HERE?"

SHE KNEW WHY SHE WAS ON DEATH ROW.

SHE DESERVED TO BE THERE.

BUT SHE WONDERED WHY I WAS EVEN IN PRISON

MUCH LESS ON DEATH ROW.

AND I SAID TO HER:

"MAYBE GOD CAN USE ME TO HELP YOU!"

AND SHE WEPT.

FROM DEEP INSIDE. SHE WEPT.

I SHARED WITH HER GOD'S LOVE IN JESUS CHRIST.

I TOLD HER GOD LOVED HER

NO MATTER WHAT THE JUDGE HAD SAID.

I LEFT HER WITH THE LOVE OF CHRIST

AND WENT BACK TO MY ROOM.

THERE I PRAYED,

AND GOD SENT ME BACK TO HER AGAIN.

AND I SAID TO HER:

"I WON'T ASK FOR YOUR CONFIDENCE IN ME. BUT SOME DAY IF YOU WANT TO TRUST ME, I WILL UNDERSTAND AND LOVE YOU, AND I WILL NEVER JUDGE OR BETRAY YOU!"

WE BECAME LOVING FRIENDS.

AND NOW IT IS TWO YEARS LATER. MY FRIEND AGAIN FACES DEATH.

SOCIETY WOULD KILL THIS LIVING SOUL.

AND IT IS I, ONLY I, WHO CAN HELP HER FIND PEACE.

BUT I CAN'T REALLY HELP HER.

ONLY THE LOVE OF JESUS CHRIST CAN HELP HER FIND THAT PEACE.

BUT THAT I WILL SHARE WITH HER

WITH ALL MY HEART!

FOR NO ONE NEEDS HIS LOVE MORE THAN SHE.

THIS LOVED ONE OF MINE WHO IS ABOUT TO DIE!

REMEMBER HER.

REMEMBER ME.

A REASON TO BE ANGRY TEACHING THE TEACHER

IN THIS PLACE OF DEATH

WE HAVE A RELIGIOUS GATHERING ONCE A WEEK.

FOR FORTY-FIVE MINUTES.

FORTY-FIVE PRECIOUS MINUTES! NO MORE!

FOR THREE YEARS NO FORMAL RELIGIOUS SERVICE WAS PROVIDED.

AND THEN I FOUND A PRISON MANUAL WHICH PROVIDED THAT DEATH ROW INMATES WOULD BE ENTITLED

TO A FORTY-FIVE MINUTE SERVICE WITH A CHAPLIN ONCE A WEEK!

I INSISTED THAT THE SERVICES BEGIN. AND THEY DID.

FOR MONTHS I WAS THE ONLY ONE WHO ATTENDED.

THE ONLY ONE!

BUT THEN ANOTHER LADY CAME.

AND FINALLY A THIRD.

WE WERE FEW IN NUMBER, BUT OH SO NEEDY.

THE CHAPLIN WHO CAME HAD A LESSON.

WRITTEN.

AND HE READ IT.

AND THEN HE PRAYED THE LORD'S PRAYER,

AND READ THE SCRIPTURE

AND THAT WAS ALL.

BUT OUR SOULS WERE NOT FED, OUR NEEDS UNMET.

WE WANTED MORE.

AND SO IN THE BOLDNESS OF CHRIST, I ASKED THIS CHAPLIN

TO SHARE FROM HIS HEART, NOT MERELY TO READ.

TO MINISTER TO US AS ONE FEELING HUMAN BEING TO ANOTHER.

WE SPENT ALMOST ALL OUR TIME READING THE SCRIPTURE.

DAY AFTER DAY.

WHAT WE NEEDED WAS SHARING FROM THE HEART.

BUT THE CHAPLIN DID NOT UNDERSTAND.

HE FELT USED, AND A COLDNESS MOVED ACROSS THE ROOM.

IN LOVE I HAD TALKED TO THE CHAPLIN ABOUT OUR NEEDS

AND HE COULD ONLY RESPOND ABOUT HIS!

PERHAPS HE DID NOT UNDERSTAND

BECAUSE HE WAS CUT OFF FROM THE NOURISHMENT OF THE SPIRIT OF GOD HIMSELF.

PERHAPS HE HAD LITTLE OF THAT SPIRITUAL TRUTH TO GIVE.

AND AGAIN, I TOLD HIM

WE WERE HUNGRY SOULS, SHEEP IN NEED OF FEEDING.

SHARE WITH US I ASKED HIM I BEGGED HIM

FROM HIS SPIRITUAL KNOWLEDGE AND INSIGHT.

HE SEEMED TO UNDERSTAND,

BUT WHEN THE SERVICE WAS OVER, HE RUSHED FROM THE ROOM WITH GREAT RELIEF.

I FOUND IT STRANGE THAT I HAD TO TEACH THE TEACHER.

I FOUND IT WAS I WHO WAS MINISTERING TO THE MINISTER.

BUT I CARRY ON, I DO WHAT I CAN.

FOR I AM FED BY THE SPIRIT OF GOD I KNOW SO WELL!

I AM NOURISHED.

I CAN TRY TO TEACH THE TEACHER.

BUT I KNOW ONLY THE SPIRIT OF GOD CAN DO THAT.

BLEEDING FROM THE HEART
A STROKE OF LOVE

AT 3:00 A.M. ONE MORNING,

THE LADIES IN PRISON WERE TALKING TO EACH OTHER.

SOME COMPLAINED BITTERLY.

OTHERS QUESTIONED.

STILL OTHERS WERE DEEPLY CONCERNED WITH THEIR FATE.

I, AWAKE, STOPPED MY READING AND LISTENED CLOSELY TO THOSE WITH BLEEDING HEARTS.

I WAITED FOR AN OPPORTUNITY TO HELP.

ONE SAW A LIGHT IN MY ROOM.

SHE CALLED FOR ME.

"MS GERALDINE, TALK TO US!"

AS I WENT TO MY WINDOW, I ASKED GOD TO GIVE ME WORDS OF TRUTH AND WISDOM.

THOSE WHO CALLED ME WERE YOUNG, SO YOUNG.

THEY REQUIRED SPECIAL ATTENTION AND CAREFUL ANSWERS.

THEY GREETED ME WARMLY AND SAID:

"MS. GERALDINE WE JUST WANT YOU TO TALK TO US".

AND I ASKED THEM WHAT THEY WISHED TO TALK ABOUT AND THEY SAID:

"MS. GERALDINE, YOU KNOW!"

IN THE QUIET COLD OF THE MORNING,

I STOOD AT MY WINDOW AND SHARED.

I TRIED WITH THE HELP OF GOD

TO TOUCH AS MANY HEARTS AS I COULD WITH STROKES OF SPIRITUAL LOVE.

I ASKED EACH OF MY LADY FRIENDS TO BE HONEST,

TO SEARCH THEIR HEARTS,

TO SEE IF THEY REALLY WANTED CHANGE,

IF THEY REALLY WANTED THINGS TO BE DIFFERENT.

IN THEIR LIVES.

IF LIFE IS TO BE MEANINGFUL, I SAID,

IT MUST HAVE A MAP, A GOAL, A PLAN.

MOST HAVE NO GOAL, NO FOCUS, NO UNDERSTANDING OF LIFE AS THEY WANT IT TO BE.

I ASKED THEM TO BE HONEST,

TO LOOK AT THEIR OWN BAD HABITS, THEIR OWN PREJUDICES.

ANY INABILITY TO SEE THEMSELVES AS THEY REALLY ARE!

AND IF, IF CHANGE IS WHAT THEY REALLY WANTED,

THEY COULD FIND THE STRENGTH FOR THAT CHANGE IN JESUS CHRIST!

BUT EACH ONE HAD TO MAKE HERSELF TOTALLY OPEN TO GOD,

TOTALLY OPEN TO HIS SPIRIT

SO THAT HE COULD HELP THEM.

AND IF EACH WOULD GIVE CONTROL OF HER LIFE TO HIM, THEN CHANGE WOULD OCCUR.

LIFE WOULD BE DIFFERENT.

GOD WOULD GIVE NEW STRENGTH, NEW COURAGE, NEW WISDOM.

FOR EVERYONE HAD FAILED.

BUT PAST FAILURE WAS NOT THE END.

FOR THERE WAS NEW LIFE IN CHRIST, A MARVELOUS NEW BEGINNING FOR THEM!

I ASKED THEM TO REMEMBER

THAT I WAS SPEAKING TO THEM FROM THE LOWEST PLACE ON EARTH.

<u>DEATH ROW!</u>

AND THAT I HAVE HAD THE STRENGTH TO GO ON,

TO CHANGE,

TO BE DIFFERENT AND GROW

BECAUSE OF THE LOVE OF CHRIST.

AND THEY LISTENED.

AND THEY LEARNED.

AND THE SPIRIT OF GOD WORKED.

AND THERE WAS HOPE.

AND THEY REMEMBERED THAT.

REMEMBER THEM.

FEEDING SHEEP

THERE WAS A LADY IN SEGREGATION.

SHE WAS SIX MONTHS PREGNANT!

ONE DAY AS I HEADED FOR MY DAILY SHOWER,

I STOPPED AND INQUIRED ABOUT HER HEALTH.

I NOTICED SHE HAD NO FOOD, NO HYGIENE SUPPLIES, NO WATER, NO TOWELS,

NOTHING.

I REPORTED THESE MISERABLE CONDITIONS TO THE OFFICER

I ASKED IF HE WOULD SO SOMETHING GOOD FOR HER.

AND FOR GOD.

I TOLD HIM I FIRMLY BELIEVED

GOD WOULD NOT FORGET SUCH A KIND ACT

AND WOULD REWARD HIS HUMAN GENEROSITY.

I TOLD HIM HE SHOULD <u>FEED THE HUNGRY</u>.

LIKE JESUS.

HE MERELY SMILED.

THEN HE PLACED HIS HANDS ON MY SHOULDERS AND SAID:

"YES MA'AM. I WILL BE BACK TO SEE YOU LATER".

WHEN HE RETURNED, I HAD PACKED MY OWN PERSONAL SUPPLIES

FOR MY FRIEND.

THE OFFICER ASKED ME WHY I DID THIS

KNOWING I WOULD NEED THESE THINGS MYSELF.

I TOLD HIM GOD WOULD SUPPLY MY NEEDS.

THAT GOD WOULD SEND SOMEONE TO DO FOR ME

AS I DID FOR HER.

I KNEW IT WOULD BE SO

FOR "I AM HIS KINGDOM KID"!

HIS CHILD.

AND THE OFFICER SAID:

"MS. GERALDINE, I BELIEVE YOU AND I AM <u>AFRAID</u> TO SAY NO. GIVE THE THINGS TO ME AND

I WILL GIVE THEM TO HER."

AND THEN I REMEMBERED THE STORY ABOUT THE WIDOW'S MITE.

LIKE HER, I WAS MAKING AN OFFERING.

IT WAS NOT IMPORTANT FOR OTHERS TO KNOW THE MEASURE OF MY GIFT.

<u>I WAS GIVING ALL THAT I COULD GIVE!</u>

GOD ALONE WOULD KNOW AND UNDERSTAND.

AND THAT WAS ALL I NEEDED.

FOR IT IS NOT WHAT WE GIVE,

BUT WHY WE GIVE.

WHEN THE OFFICER GAVE MY FRIEND MY PACKAGE, SHE HOLLERED:

"THANK YOU MS. GERALDINE!"

MY HEART SANG.

I HAD DONE GOD'S WILL FOR HER.

AND I HAD OPENED THE DOOR FOR SPIRITUAL CONTACT

WITH THE OFFICER.

AND I KNEW HE WOULD RETURN.

FOR ME TO MINISTER TO HIM!

HE REMEMBERED.

AND HE CAME BACK!

WILL THE SHADOW MOVE FROM ME

AN OFFICER CAME TO MY CELL ONE DAY.

HE BROUGHT THREE LETTERS.

ONE HAD NO NAME. NO ADDRESS.

IT WAS SIMPLY ADDRESSED TO MS. GERALDINE.

THE LETTER WAS ANOTHER CRY FOR HELP

FROM A HURTING SOUL.

THE YOUNG LADY TOLD ME

WHEN WE FIRST MET,

SHE DID NOT BELIEVE IN GOD.

AFTER THAT, EACH DAY IN THE RECREATION HOUR,

I HAD TOLD HER OFTEN ABOUT MY LORD'S CHARACTER

AND HOW HIS LOVE HAD KEPT ME

THROUGH MY DIFFICULT JOURNEY.

I KNEW SHE WAS LISTENING.

I KNEW SHE NEEDED MORE.

HER LIFE WAS FULL OF HURT.

SHE NEEDED MORE THAN I COULD GIVE HER.

SHE NEEDED HIM!

BUT SHE WAS LIKE SO MANY WOMEN

INCARCERATED FOR YEARS.

THERE WAS NO HOPE, SHE BELIEVED.

DRUGS TO GET HER THROUGH THE DAY.

THAT WAS ALL THAT MATTERED!

ANY TEMPORARY RELIEF. ANY QUICK FIX!

ESCAPE FROM THEIR ANGER, THEIR HATE,

THEIR DESIRE FOR VENGEANCE,

THEIR DESIRE TO RETURN EVIL FOR EVIL.

BUT THE STRONGEST DRUG CAN NEVER DO THAT.

BUT THERE IS STILL HOPE.

EVEN WITHOUT DRUGS.

EVEN SHE HAD HOPED FOR SOMETHING BETTER. WITHOUT DRUGS.

SHE LISTENED AS I SHARED.

AND I PRAYED SHE WOULD HEAR.

FOR I KNEW THAT WHEN GODLY SEEDS ARE PLANTED,

THERE IS ALWAYS A HARVEST.

HIS WORD NEVER RETURNS VOID!

HER LETTER WAS SO REAL, SO HONEST,

FROM A HURTING SOUL BATTLING THE DEVIL.

HOPING, EVEN PRAYING THAT THINGS WOULD WORK TOGETHER FOR GOOD IN HER LIFE.

A LETTER FROM A LADY WHOM GOD LOVES.

Hello my friend, Ms. Geraldine

Time gives me the pleasure to send a friendly message your way in hopes that it finds you, as always, doing well in every respect. As for me, I'm okay. I am in a thinking stage right now. You probably can tell for I have just now gotten around to writing you, my friend, this much belated message. I miss time with you in recreation like we had together back in 1992 and 1993. We were able to talk more and you had given me so much insight. Thank you! Unfortunately, I don't retain wisdom well when the devil in me takes over. No one knows, but for every outburst or altercation that I get into, I later cry and then pray for strength and forgiveness. But what's the use if I only explode again the next day. Obviously, I'm not hearing the word. Yet I do understand and feel every word that I read in the Bible.

I feel so evil, bitter, hateful and vengeful to anyone that I believe is oppressing me. Or tries to cause me harm. Some people think I'm nuts-insane. But no, I am very sane! I have evil, satan in me and I don't know how to get him out. I even wrote the Chaplin a month ago for help. She brought me three books to read. I've read two and enjoyed them. But still, something is not clicking. I still hate the staff of the prison and the petty inmates. I think constantly of ways to get even and it bothers me. I read Psalm 37:8 and Hebrews 11. I read the Old Testament to get even better understanding of creation and life in the beginning as a whole. I really am trying, but I just can't tolerate the wrongs done to me and, as always, I fall in God's eyes.

So many think I'm mean and evil, but they don't know me. All I want is fairness. But I think I'm fighting a losing battle. I will write again when I get more paper. That will be soon I promise. But I need to read my Bible because I do believe that one day, something will click and it will all come together.

I love you.

Your friend.

ANOTHER LETTER FROM MY FRIEND

ANOTHER LETTER FROM MY FRIEND.

THE ONE WHO DOES NOT BELIEVE IN GOD.

OR AT LEAST AT ONE TIME, SHE DIDN'T.

SINCE HER FIRST LETTER TO ME, I HAVE MINISTERED TO HER.

I HAD ASKED THAT SHE BE ALLOWED TO READ MY WRITINGS.

PERMISSION WAS GRANTED!

MY HEART LEAPED FOR JOY!

AFTER SHE READ MY WRITINGS, SHE WROTE ME AGAIN.

HOW FAR SHE HAS COME!

HOW THRILLED I AM TO HAVE BEEN ABLE TO HELP HER.

ANOTHER LETTER FROM MY FRIEND!

Hello my friend,

Please excuse the paper. It's all I have at the moment. Time has again permitted me the pleasure of sending a friendly message your way. I pray that all is well for you. You certainly deserve the best in life because you are the best (smile). I am fine today. Just a bit sad and in search for some peace.

I really enjoyed your writings. It was very interesting reading which did bring me enlightenment. As you know, I felt I suffered relentlessly. I felt I was persecuted and unjustly treated. But I know the suffering of Jesus was much greater. The Bible never came alive for me. It was always just a story being told or read. But your writings have brought Jesus off the printed pages of the Bible for me today. And they really made me think how good he is and how others made him suffer.

I am an incarcerated mother. And I truly believe that the child suffers more than me which is unfortunate because he has done nothing. Even though this is my second time, I am very remorseful. My son is no longer a little baby and he is at the age where he needs his mom the most. Especially since he doesn't have a dad. Next year when I go home, he will be in eighth grade and I'll have time to work with him and prepare him for high school. Which I know he would never survive without his mom. I must make his life better than mine. I only have one child so I only have one chance. I am determined not to ruin it. Not only do I need to put the church in my life. But I need to put it in his life as well. That's probably why life is such a struggle for me because I'm attempting to live it without God!

I hope that I can hold on to my desire to change and find God no matter how many times I fail or lose my composure. I confess one thing to you, Ms. Geraldine. I really don't know where to begin picking up the pieces of my life, or how to begin my search for Christ. I am now reading the scriptures in hopes that they will soften my heart. For I agree with you that I need a plan for my life to be successful at anything in life. There must be a plan, a map, a blueprint so that we can stay on course. So that's what I need to concentrate on so that I don't always fail or fall short. I'm reading Isaiah this evening from the beginning. So far I have made it to Chapter 23 and I've obtained biblical knowledge for one, but most importantly, I have received the message to wash away my evil ways. I know it will not be easy because Satan is a working force in me.

I will close now but I will be in touch.

Love,

Your friend

P.S. I no longer take prescription drugs. I gave them up because I want to see if I can live my life without them and instead, with spiritual strength. I don't regret it!

THE VALUE OF HUMAN LIFE

I BELIEVE THAT IF WE SEE EVIL AND DO NOTHING WE ARE GUILTY.

WE ARE CONSPIRATORS.

WE ARE AS GUILTY AS THE ONE WHO DOES THE CRIME.

RECENTLY, I LISTENED TO A DISCUSSION ABOUT <u>GANGS AND DRUGS</u>.

SOME OF THE LADIES FELT THAT GANGS WERE WRONG.

BUT MANY FELT HELPLESS TO RESIST THE DEMANDS OF A GANG.

THAT POWER CAME FROM THE GANGS, STRONGER THAN THEY WERE.

BUT THEY WOULD NEVER ADMIT THIS WEAKNESS AND ASK FOR HELP.

INSTEAD, THEY DEVELOPED AN ATTITUDE, TOUGH AND INDEPENDENT.

BUT A GREAT NEED WAS THERE.

SOME FELT PLEASURE GETTING AWAY WITH SOMETHING.

BUT OTHERS WERE WEARY, SO WEARY OF CRIME AND CRIMINAL BEHAVIOR.

THEY WANTED SOMETHING DIFFERENT.

SOME OF THE BLACK LADIES REFLECTED ON THE HARD TIMES OF THEIR PARENTS.

PROBLEMS SEEMED TO PASS FROM ONE GENERATION TO ANOTHER.

STILL OTHERS BLAMED WHITES FOR THEIR PROBLEMS.

AND OTHERS STILL CLAIMED THEY HAD NO PERSONAL RESPONSIBILITY FOR THEIR CRIMINAL ACTIONS.

SOME KNEW OF NO WAY OUT.

ALL WISHED TO IMPROVE THEIR LIVES, BUT ONLY IF IT COST THEM NOTHING.

THEY WANTED GAIN WITHOUT PAIN.

THESE BLACK WOMEN WERE ANGERED AND OUTRAGED IF ANYONE SPOKE ABOUT CRIMES COMMITTED BY

WHITES UPON BLACKS.

BUT THEY SEEMED BLINDED WHEN THE SUBJECT DEALT WITH BLACKS KILLING BLACKS.

OR BLACKS RUINING THE LIVES OF BLACK CHILDREN BECAUSE OF DRUGS AND THE CRIMINAL ACTIVITY OF

GANGS.

BUT THEY ALL UNDERSTOOD PAIN.

PAIN, FOR THEM, WAS SYNONYMOUS WITH LIFE ITSELF.

THEY SEEMED TO UNDERSTAND THE PAIN OF CHRIST, HIS CRUEL DEATH ON THE CROSS.

THAT MADE SENSE. THEY UNDERSTOOD HIS SUFFERING.

BUT AFTER YEARS OF THEIR OWN PAIN, IT SEEMED AS THOUGH THEY HAD GIVEN UP

NO LONGER WILLING TO FIGHT TO OVERCOME.

THEY FELT PART OF A LOST GENERATION. UNWILLING TO TRY TO CHANGE ANYTHING.

THEY SAW LITTLE VALUE IN HUMAN LIFE.

AND THEN I HEARD LATIN LADIES SPEAK.

THEY THOUGHT THERE WAS REAL POWER IN GANGS.

REAL POWER IN USING DRUGS.

ONE LADY INDICATED SHE LOVED THE POWER SHE FELT OVER OTHER PEOPLE BECAUSE OF HER POSITION IN

THE GANG.

SHE SET RULES AND OTHERS FOLLOWED.

BUT SHE HAD NO SENSE OF VALUE FOR HUMAN LIFE.

IT WAS ALL ABOUT PRIDE. AND POWER

IT WAS OBVIOUS THERE WAS A HUNGER FOR LEADERSHIP, FOR ROLE MODELS.

BUT THE LEADERS THEY FOLLOWED WERE LOSERS WITHOUT A FUTURE.

THEY TALKED ABOUT THE LAW OF THE STREET:

<u>KILL OR BE KILLED</u>!

THAT'S WHY THERE IS NO END TO THE KILLING.

BUT BENEATH ALL THE TALK WERE SOULS CRYING OUT FOR RESCUE.

RESCUE FROM THE LAW OF SIN AND DEATH.

HOW I LONGED TO HELP THEM, TO SHARE WITH THEM THE LOVE OF CHRIST.

I KNOW HOW MUCH THEY WANT AND NEED THAT LOVE.

THEY SING THE OLD TUNE, GANGS AND DRUGS.

BUT THE END OF THAT SONG IS DEATH AND DESTRUCTION.

THERE IS HOPE BUT IT IS SO HARD FOR THEM TO SEE.

THE HOPE IS IN <u>HIM</u>. WE MUST REMEMBER THAT.

REMEMBER THEM.

REMEMBER ME.

MINISTRY IN A COFFIN

I AM A MINISTER!

ON DEATH ROW.

I HAVE HAD MY PULPIT HERE

AMONG THE CONDEMNED FOR FIVE YEARS.

I AM CALLED TO PREACH BECAUSE THERE IS NO OTHER.

IN MY PRISON CHURCH, THERE ARE NO ROBES, NO RITUALS TO GUIDE US.

SOMETIMES ONLY ONE ATTENDS.

WE FOCUS ON THE BASICS OF OUR LORD'S TEACHINGS

AND WE GROW TOGETHER.

THERE IS NO ONE ELSE TO HELP US. BUT <u>HE</u> IS MORE THAN ENOUGH.

SOMETIMES WE LOOK TO THE CHURCH OUTSIDE FOR HELP.

SOME HELP, SOME DON'T.

SOME DO IT FOR THE RIGHT REASONS,

SOME FOR THE WRONG REASONS.

BUT THE NEED GOES ON, THE WORKERS FEW.

BUT WE, THE WORKERS, CONTINUE TO CALL OUT FROM DEATH ROW.

FOR HELP

FROM OUR BROTHERS AND SISTERS IN THE CHURCH OUT THERE.

BUT WE REALIZE

SISTERS IN THE LORD OUT THERE OFTEN DO NOT RECOGNIZE US

AS SISTERS IN THE LORD IN HERE.

SOME THAT DO COME

SOME ENTER THE PRISON WITHOUT HUMILITY OR LOVE.

SOME COME AND NEVER RETURN.

SOME CARE FOR THE MOMENT BUT SOON FORGET.

WE ARE HURT.

HOW WRONG BECAUSE OUR SAVIOR NEVER LEFT US ALONE,

HE NEVER FORGOT US.

EVEN WHEN HE LEFT, HE SENT HIS SPIRIT.

AND SO WE ARE NOT ALONE NO MATTER WHAT.

NO MATTER WHERE.

WE STAND TOGETHER IN THIS CEMENT COFFIN

THIS CONDEMNED GRAVEYARD

NURTURED BY THE SPIRIT OF GOD, THE COMFORTER.

AND WE CONTINUE TO REACH OUT TO OUR BROTHERS AND SISTERS OUTSIDE.

BUT KNOWING THAT EVEN IF THEY FORSAKE US, GOD NEVER WILL!

GOD NEVER LEAVES ANYONE ALONE

EVEN ON DEATH ROW.

PLEASE REMEMBER THAT.

PHYSICAL BRAVERY AND MORAL COURAGE

SEE THE DIFFERENCE, MY FRIENDS,

BETWEEN PHYSICAL BRAVERY AND MORAL COURAGE.

PHYSICAL BRAVERY IS BUT TEMPORARY.

IT MEETS CHALLENGES, IT EXPENDS ITS ENERGY, AND IT IS <u>GONE</u>.

BUT <u>MORAL</u> COURAGE

THAT HAS FIBER AND SUBSTANCE WHICH ENDURE.

WE FIGHT THE FIGHT OF FAITH WITH THIS ENDURING MORAL COURAGE.

IT SUSTAINS US.

IT DOES NOT ALLOW US TO SUCCUMB.

IT PUTS DOWN SELF INTEREST, PRIDE OR DESIRE FOR FAME.

IT ENERGIZES US TO DO OUR VERY BEST.

ALL OF OUR LIVES HAVE BEEN CONTAMINATED BY SIN.

WE ARE CONSTANTLY CALLED UPON TO CHOSE BETWEEN RIGHT AND WRONG,

GOOD AND EVIL.

WE CAN ONLY DO THE RIGHT WHEN WE ARE FILLED WITH MORAL COURAGE

THE COURAGE OF JESUS CHRIST.

THE HEROISM OF THE MOMENT MAY SEEM QUITE WONDERFUL, SPECTACULAR.

AND SOMETIMES IT IS!

BUT THE REALLY HARD THING, FIGHTING EVIL FOR A <u>LIFETIME</u>

CAN ONLY BE DONE WITH LASTING <u>MORAL</u> <u>COURAGE</u>.

<u>LOVE</u> IS THE SOURCE OF MORAL COURAGE.

THE GREATER THE LOVE, THE GREATER THE COURAGE.

AND THE BETTER, STRONGER SERVANT.

I AM HIS SERVANT.

I AM FILLED WITH <u>HIS</u> LOVE AND MORAL COURAGE.

I AM MS. GERALDINE.

GERALDINE SMITH!

I AM A RESIDENT OF DEATH ROW.

BUT I AM REALLY A COURAGEOUS KINGDOM PERSON.

STAND WITH ME.

REMEMBER ME!

THE HEART OF A YOUNG GENTLEMAN

I HAVE A SON.

HE IS NINE YEARS OLD.

WE HAVE BEEN SEPARATED OUR ENTIRE LIVES!

I SEE HIM ONCE OR TWICE A YEAR.

THAT'S ALL!

HE LIVES WITH MY FAMILY.

HE HAS BEEN SICK MOST OF HIS LIFE.

BUT HE IS WELL EDUCATED, WELL BEHAVED.

HE IS MANNERLY AND RESPECTFUL.

HE IS A GIFTED SPEAKER WHO LOVES TO PICK THE SUBJECT.

ONE OF HIS MOST STRIKING QUALITY IS HIS ABILITY TO <u>LISTEN</u>.

HE REALLY LISTENS!

<u>BUT ABOVE ALL</u> HE IS COMPASSIONATE, <u>LOVING</u>

EVEN TO THOSE WHO HATE ME, HIS MOTHER.

GOD HAS KEPT HIM AND BLESSED HIM

THIS MY BELOVED SON.

ONCE MY SON CAME TO VISIT ME.

WHILE GOING THROUGH SECURITY, MY SON IDENTIFIED A SUPERVISOR AS A MAN OF AUTHORITY BY HIS DRESS.

MY SON ASKED THE SERGEANT WHETHER OR NOT HE HAD AUTHORITY OVER OTHER PEOPLE.

THE SERGEANT SAID YES.

GOOD, SAID MY SON.

THEN HE SAID:

"WILL YOU HELP ME?"

AND THE SERGEANT SAID YES. TO WHICH MY SON REPLIED:

"SINCE YOU TELL OTHER PEOPLE HERE WHAT TO DO, WILL YOU PLEASE HELP ME BY TELLING THEM TO LET MY MOTHER GO HOME WITH ME FOR A DAY?

"MY SON THEN EXPLAINED TO THE FRIENDLY SERGEANT HOW GOOD AND KIND HIS MOTHER WAS TO EVERYBODY.

AT THIS, THE SERGEANT BECAME VERY EMOTIONAL AND COULD NOT CONTINUE THE SECURITY PROCEDURE.

DAYS LATER, THE SERGEANT CAME TO ME AND APOLOGIZED FOR NOT BEING ABLE TO CONTAIN HIS EMOTIONS.

FOR HE HAD WITNESSED SOMETHING VERY SPECIAL ABOUT MY SON.

IT HAD MADE A LASTING IMPACT ON HIM.

HE SAW HOW MUCH MY SON LOVED ME.

EVEN TODAY, THAT SERGEANT GETS EMOTIONAL IF THAT EXPERIENCE IS BROUGHT UP.

HE REMEMBERS.

<u>OUT OF THE MOUTHS OF BABES!</u>

MY BELOVED SON WAS ONLY FIVE YEARS OLD. BUT HE WAS FILLED WITH THE WISDOM OF THE HOLY SPIRIT.

HOW I LOVED HIM FOR WHAT HE DID!

MY SON'S NAME IS LOUIA.

HE REMEMBERS ME.

WILL YOU?

GIVING BACK FOR BETTERNESS

A BAR OF SOAP

"WILL YOU GIVE TO MAKE THINGS BETTERS?" "IF SO, THEN WHAT WILL YOU GIVE?" I ASK THESE QUESTIONS OF MY FELLOW INCARCERATED WOMEN.

AT FIRST, THESE LADIES WERE PUZZLED. GIVE, GIVE WHAT THEY ASKED, AND FOR WHAT? I WAS NOT SURPRISED AT THE ANSWER FOR MOST PEOPLE FEEL THAT WAY. BUT MY FEMALE FRIENDS IN PRISON REALLY HAVE NOTHING TO GIVE. GIVING NOTHING MEANS HAVING NOTHING, TO THEM. BUT IN ALL CASES, AND IN OURS TOO, WE OURSELVES HAVE NOTHING BECAUSE WE REFUSE TO GIVE OR SHARE EVEN THAT WHICH WE HAVE!

I ASKED THESE LADIES TO REFLECT ON A STRIKING, LOVING ACT OF JESUS. THE MASTER, THE SON OF GOD, WASHED HIS OWN DISCIPLES FEET! I BELIEVE THIS SPECIAL ACT OF AFFECTION IS THE ULTIMATE LESSON IN HUMILITY. AS THESE LADIES REFLECTED ON THE ACTION OF JESUS, SOME THOUGHT IT STRANGE WHILE OTHERS THOUGHT IT WONDERFUL AND DEAR. SOME WOMEN ADMITTED THAT THEY COULD SEE THEIR OWN SELFISHNESS AND PRIDE MORE CLEARLY. OTHERS FELT THAT EVEN THOUGH THEY, THEMSELVES, HAD NOTHING, YET IT WAS STILL DEMEANING TO BEND DOWN AND WASH THE FEET OF SOMEONE ELSE. BUT THE LESSON IS THE MORE HUMBLE WE ARE, THE LESS OF OURSELVES, THE MORE ROOM FOR THE LOVE OF GOD. THE MORE HUMBLE WE ARE, THE MORE WILLING WE ARE TO DO FOR OTHERS.

I REMINDED THEM OF <u>MOTHER YORK</u>. SHE BROUGHT THE INMATES BARS OF SOAP, TUBES OF TOOTHPASTE, SHAMPOO AND OTHER HUMBLE, BUT SUCH NECESSARY THINGS. SHE DID THAT WHEN NO ONE ELSE DID. AND MOTHER YORK TOLD THEM AS SHE GAVE, IN HER SOFT, LOVING, FIRM

VOICE, HOW MUCH SHE LOVED THEM AND HOW MUCH GOD LOVED THEM. BUT NONE OF THEM WHO RECEIVED SAID THAT UPON THEIR RELEASE THEY WOULD AID THIS KIND AND LOVING LADY IN ORDER TO GIVE BACK AND MAKE THINGS BETTER FOR SOMEONE ELSE AS SHE HAD DONE FOR THEM. NONE OF THEM!

FOR SOME REASON, THESE LADIES FELT THAT ONE MUST BE RICH OR HAVE AN ABUNDANCE TO GIVE. OR TO AT LEAST GIVE ANYTHING WORTHWHILE. MOST ADMITTED THAT GIVING SMALL THINGS HAD NEVER EVEN CROSSED THEIR MINDS. THEY HAD NEVER SEEN THE VALUE OF GIVING ANYTHING, NO MATTER HOW SMALL, IN LOVE.

GIVE AND IT SHALL BE GIVEN BACK TO YOU. GIVING IS THE GREATEST PLEASURE. EVEN THOSE WITH THE HARDEST OF HEARTS LEARNED SOMETHING THAT DAY. THEY LEARNED THAT NO MATTER HOW LITTLE THEY HAD, IF THEY GAVE JUST A LITTLE, LITTLE IS MUCH WHEN GOD IS IN IT!

WHAT REALLY MATTERS IN LIFE

JOY!

WHEREVER I AM

I AM CONTENT.

IN HIS LOVE.

I LIVE WITH DEATH.

IN A CEMENT COFFIN.

AND YET I AM FULL OF JOY!

FOR JOY COMES NOT FROM THE THINGS AROUND ME.

JOY RESIDES IN MY SOUL!

NO MATTER HOW GREAT THE TROUBLE AROUND ME, I FIND MY JOY IN HIM!

UNSPEAKABLE JOY!

AND THAT JOY MAKES ME SO CONTENT AT PEACE.

CONTENT TO DO GOD'S WORK IN PRISON.

CONTENT TO DO GOD'S WORK AMONG THE CONDEMNED.

THE FORSAKEN. THE JOYLESS.

CONTENT TO PREACH THE WORDS OF ETERNAL LIFE IN THE NEVER ENDING PRESENCE OF DEATH.

I AM FULL OF HIS JOY!

FULL!

I AM CONTENT TO BE WHO I AM.

WHERE I AM.

HIS JOY IS ALL THAT MATTERS.

I REMEMBER THAT EVERY DAY!

DO YOU?

A BITTER CUP

PRISON BONDAGE IS MY PLIGHT.

NO WORDS CAN DESCRIBE THE HORROR OF MY LIFE.

MY CUP IS BITTER.

SO OFTEN I BEG FOR MERCY.

I CRY TO GOD FOR HELP

LIKE ABEL'S BLOOD FROM THE GROUND.

I DO THAT IN SILENCE,

IT IS BETWEEN <u>HIM</u> AND ME.

BUT WHEN I SPEAK OUT, MY <u>EVERY WORD</u> IS A LIVING TESTIMONY TO MY FAITH IN GOD!

AND I SHARE THAT I AM A CHRISTIAN

SAVED BY GRACE!

HOWEVER MUCH I HURT, MY TESTIMONY WILL BE STRONG FOR HIM.

FOR I LIVE IN HIS WORD

AND I WILL SPEAK HIS WORDS.

I AM INTOXICATED. SPIRITUALLY HIGH WITH HIS LOVE!

AND I WILL SHARE THAT WITH MY MOUTH.

I WILL NEVER BE DISCOURAGED.

YOU MAY HEAR ME CRY. WHEN I HURT.

YOU MAY HEAR ME BEG FOR MERCY.

FOR HELP.

YOU MAY KNOW MY WEAKNESS,

MY <u>PAIN</u>.

BUT THE WORDS FROM MY LIPS WILL ONLY GIVE PRAISE TO MY LORD!

MINE IS <u>NOT</u> A BITTER CUP.

I DRINK EVERY DAY FROM <u>HIS</u> CUP OF LOVE AND GRACE.

REMEMBER ME!